IN TRANSIT

Tshenuwani Simon Farisani

In Transit

Between the Image of God and the Image of Man

WILLIAM B. EERDMANS PUBLISHING COMPANY
GRAND RAPIDS, MICHIGAN

AFRICA WORLD PRESS, INC.
TRENTON, NEW JERSEY

255 Jefferson Ave. S.E., Grand Rapids, Mich., 49503
First published 1990 jointly by Eerdmans and Africa World Press, Inc.,
P.O. Box 1892, Trenton, N.J.

Printed in the United States of America

Library of Congress Cataloging-in-Publication Data

Farisani, Tshenuwani Simon.
In transit: between the image of God and the image of man / Tshenuwani Simon Farisani.
p. cm.
1. Farisani, Tshenuwani Simon. 2. Evangelical Lutheran Church in Southern Africa—Clergy—Biography. 3. Lutheran Church—South Africa—Clergy—Biography. 4. South Africa—Race relations. 5. Race relations—Religious aspects—Christianity. 6. Apartheid—South Africa. I. Title.
BX8080.F35A3 1990
284.1'092—dc20
[B] 90–36509
CIP

Eerdmans ISBN 0–8028–0438–1
Africa World ISBN 0-86543-207-4

Contents

Preface

God created humanity in his own image—whatever that means! In Egypt, Pharaoh the King tried hard to re-create Israel in the image of a lesser god. He failed. In the desert, in the crucible of hunger and thirst, in the face of suffering and death, the clay that Pharaoh used to create slave women and slave men God used to create a great nation that would become the vessel of salvation to the human race. Who would have guessed, as Israel stood caught between the Red Sea and Pharaoh's army, between God's loving and the slave drivers' exploiting intentions, in transit from slavery to freedom, that Israel would one day boast a King David sitting on a God-ordained throne?

When crushed by Assyria,
When enslaved by Babylon,
When scattered by Rome,
Whose image emerged, God's or the oppressor's?

The world's black communities know what it is

- to be less than God intended;
- to earn less for the same hours and skills;
- to come first and get service last;
- to invest a smile and earn a frown;
- to cry for a living wage and get a killing bullet;
- to stretch out a loving hand and be accused of impertinence;
- to keep to themselves and be accused of black racism;

- to call for affirmative action and be faulted for reverse racism;
- to serve the Supreme Being in their own ways and be accused of idolatry;
- to convert to Christianity and be told that Christ has no cure for racism.

Stranded between God-God and Human-God!

In South Africa, whose creature is

- the Aborigine?
- the Native?
- the Kaffir?
- the Bantu?
- the Non-European?
- the Non-White?
- the Cooperative?
- the Plural?

In whose image? This list—and it does not pretend to exhaust the racist vocabulary—catalogs the "existential evolution" of the "people of color" between 1652 and today, perhaps beyond. Existence from racist-made ape to human-made subhuman; from nonexistence to peripheral existence; from home to homelessness; from small boy to big boy; from moaning to mourning; from he/she-being to it-being; from woman to Bantu female.

Between Heaven's Will and Pretoria's Whim!

When Pretoria imposes restrictions and banning orders on people, they cease to move: they become soulless souls like Adam and Eve before they received the breath of life. The spirit says, "Speak up!" The ghost of Jimmy Kruger says, "Biko, shut up!" The spirit says to the oppressed: "Mandela says, 'Fight for freedom. Freedom is in your hands. In the land of Africa!'" Botha says, "Mandela, you shall know your place."

Has Pretoria failed to re-create black humanity in the image of Dr. Hendrik Verwoerd? Has Bantu education failed to mold a subservient black youth and nation whose aspirations would not interfere with the "green pastures" reserved for whites? It does not take much listening to hear the cries for "equal education for equal people," "all schools for all people," "all God's beaches for all God's people," "all buses and trains for all commuters," "all hospitals for all patients," "all ballot boxes for all colors," and "all power to all the people!" Is this God's image re-emerging?

When I received a twelve-hour in-transit visa from the God of Internal Affairs in February 1987, I drove the more or less six-hundred-kilometer stretch in about four and a half hours, at a speed between 160 and 180 kilometers-per-hour to Jan Smuts Airport in Kempton Park, outside Johannesburg. For the first time I learned at close range how dangerous it is to be a human-being-in-transit: it is to be no-human-being-at-all. When on August 3, 1987, in the United States, I received a re-entry visa in transit for twelve hours between Jan Smuts and my home at Beuster—to live under the same restrictions—the message came home solid and clear: In God I am; in transit I am *persona non grata.*

In April 1978, the insensitive hand of Jimmy Kruger left my hopes in a state of trauma (see my book *Diary from a South African Prison,* a word to the reader). And in a more cruel, more insensitive fashion, Adriaan Vlok, "reformer" President F. W. de Klerk's minister of "law and order," in a meeting with a delegation of our Lutheran Church—Bishops S. E. Serote and Manas Buthelezi, General Secretary Mervin D. Assur, and church council member Z. Z. Mashao—on September 22, 1989, hit a final nail into my coffin: "Farisani must be equally sensitive. The way he addresses people. If this happens I have to detain him again. I do not want to create any expectation in the delegation's mind" (see full details of the meeting in Appendix C).

I want to respond to the minister of "law and order": Our

people have always rejected your apartheid god and all it stands for, and so do I. Rolihlahla Nelson Mandela, and all freedom- and justice-loving people before him and after him, have suffered with him unmitigated, insensitive, racist state terrorism. It was not because they were insensitive; on the contrary, it was just because they cared and were selflessly sensitive—perhaps too sensitive—to the suffering of their fellow oppressed. God and God's people are always sensitive to the needs and cries of their homeless, orphans, widows, strangers, prisoners, hungry, thirsty, landless, exploited, oppressed, tortured, disappeared, assassinated, vigilanted, restricted, banned, exiled, dispossessed, disenfranchised, dehumanized, fragmented, marginalized, hunted, executed, abused, neglected. And you are the best qualified to complete that list, Adriaan Vlok!

But I want to plead guilty, Mr. Vlok: *With thirty-three million of our oppressed people we have fought apartheid in the past, we are fighting it now, and we shall fight it in the future.* It is not the liberation movement that is insensitive; it is the South African Offense Force. It is not SWAPO that is insensitive; it is *Koevoet.*[1] It is not the ANC that must renounce violence; it is the racist apartheid regime. It is not I that must stop inciting the people against degrading oppression; it is the racist regime that you, Adriaan Vlok, represent that must now stop insulting our humanity and playing games with the black citizenship of South Africa. It is not the World Alliance of Reformed Churches that must reform its theology of race; it is the White Dutch Reformed Churches that must renounce their heresy and find a way to bring back to life:

- David Webster—assassins unknown(?)
- Dulcie September—case under investigation(?)
- bombed Khotso house—no leads yet (?)
- malnourished children—only enough food for export(?)

1. *Koevoet:* special racist-terrorist unit of the South African Defense Force (SADF) set against SWAPO's liberation struggle.

This book is dedicated to my Reggy Regina Nemaembeni Farisani and all women and men whose spouses "disappeared" on occasion or forever. Without their support and courage, our souls would have long ago been crushed by the oppressor and the dust used to create homeland bishops and cabinet ministers for religious and peripheral affairs. *A NI RI TSHILELI NDOU!*

Berkeley, California, USA Tshenuwani Simon Farisani
November 1989

Prologue: I Have Been to the Palace

It is the year 1600 after the birth of the colorless son who now sits comfortably at the right hand of his colorful father. Old Van Riebeeck has just arrived this morning from a night-long trip. Back in the land of snow, surrounded by those like snow, around an evening fire, O.V.R.[1] makes his unbiased report:

"The place is far, beyond the seventh cloud. I met him face to face. We are chosen and called for a mission beyond the oceans. I am too old for the task. But my son Jan will build on the foundation of my dream. Among you are men and women of vision and valor who will go with my son.

"When you dock, you will be required to speak a new language, related to your own but reshaped by the new environment. You will also be required to cultivate new relationships between yourselves and those who never saw snow and are unlike snow. They have no ambition, they have no dreams; they have no values, they have no norms. They are a strange breed, and they breed without limit. Everyone among them is a god, but there is no god among them. They do not like strangers, and they do not like one another. They like to kill; they drink blood. When he was routed from heaven, Satan immediately created his own image. You will meet his images there. I do not think they can be converted; but like their father, they can be defeated. Whatever is left of Satan's soul, that they have inherited in every respect.

1. O.V.R.: Old Van Riebeeck.

"Whatever you are willing to give them, let it not be your love; whatever you are willing to share with them, let it not be your power or your daughters; however high you want to raise them, let your waist be the limit. Always stand tall above them. Dwarf them. Tower above them. Whichever of their trees grows exceptionally tall in intellect and in physique, that you must cut to size or completely down. Always remember that, just as their father is banned from the palace above, likewise his descendants must never take the seat of honor among you. Every attempt on their part to climb the ladder must remind you of their father's attempted coup against the king above. Like father, like son.

"To use them and avoid contamination at the same time, you will need separate structures at social, political, economic, and spiritual levels. While I never saw one room for them in our father's house, it will not be a bad idea to keep them chasing after his shadow if this will help subdue their animal and satanic instincts. If some claim conversion, drench them in mosquito-infested waters. You may even give them stale bread and cheap wine, but never dine and wine with them. Have you ever seen a tree with ox horns or a fish with flowers? Fauna and flora—they are not one body. Can you transplant Satan's nose onto Christ's face? Words have power; phrases are power; language creates. It is as powerful as God.

"I have been instructed to tell you to speak one language among yourselves and another with them. Among yourselves you will be *broers* and brothers; *broederbonds* and brotherhoods; *ooms* and uncles; *tanies* and aunties; *oumas* and grandmothers; *oupa grootjies* and great grandpas. You will call each other *meneer* and sir, *mevrou* and madam. When you speak of and to them, here is the vocabulary: boy and *kaffir, piccanin* and kaffirmaid, *bobbejaan* and baboon, *domkop* and dunderhead, *madala* and old fool. They will always speak to you as if you were a third person, saying: Baas and Missis, Oubaas and Oumissis, Basie and Nonnie, Kleinbaas and Kleinmissis. They will speak of themselves in derogatory terms, saying: *die ander boy,* or the other boy; *die missis se kaffertjie,* or the missus' small kaffir. Keep things this way to keep yourselves pure. I come from there. I am from the palace. The maker wants things done as instructed. If you want to go, you must listen; if not, stay at home. Remember to respect me, your father; I also respect my God. Are you ready? The ships are waiting for you."

* * * * *

The day is April 6, 1652. Three ships, *Dromedaris*, *Reyger*, and *De Goede Hoop*, dock at the Cape, Africa's southern toe. This will be a halfway station between Europe and Asia, says the Dutch East India Company. Only small gardens, orchards, and farms will be cultivated to provide fresh vegetables, fruits, grains, meat, and water for ships in transit.

Before sunset the passengers would force their way through customs without entry visas, pushing into wider South Africa, forcing native Africans into apartheid boats in transit to Transkei, Bophuthatswana, Venda, Ciskei, Kwandebele, Qwa Qwa, Gazankulu, Lebowa, Kwazulu, and Kangwane.

In 1976, *Boat Transkei* would dock at Umtata; in 1977, *Boat Bophuthatswana* at Mmabatho; in 1979, *Boat Venda* at Thohoyandou; and in 1981, *Boat Ciskei* at Bisho, thanks to the skillful skippers, their excellencies Matanzima, Mangope, Mphephu, and Sebe. By decree and proclamation, they would take with them millions of forced passengers into homeland dead seas. The other six boats would be forced to follow suit, even if they had to sail through Blood Sea. On the surface, Tshaka's descendant is not eager to travel down the steep road to the salt sea. It is rumored that his reliable informants have warned him that there is no life in the Dead Sea, but that opportunists can float on the cursed waters and remain respectable in Washington and at 10 Downing Street. Reliable sources say he will float on this lowest lake below sea level for as long as it pays to be all things to all people. His friends add that he knows he will have to dock at Nongoma sooner or later, or accept a peripheral role in a national statutory council pot in which Cook Botha prepares *eintopf*, mixing fish, chicken, pork, beef, oysters, crayfish, mushrooms, vegetables, kangaroo steak, presumably without integrating racial flavors and risking one dominating minority taste. Prophets and diviners say Tshaka and Dingane are turning in their graves, calling upon the spirits of those who fell at Blood River to stop the betrayal of their proud history.

Our evidence is that the spirit of true Uhuru has revisited the Dead Sea capitals and is already perched on the decks of the six other boats in transit. Bones are coming together: some skeletons are again covered in flesh. They are dreaming dreams and seeing visions. Nebuchadnezzar and his governors are hearing discomforting songs of the resurrected: *Mayibuye Afrika!* Rolihlahla Mandela, show us the way to freedom! *Asikhathali noma siyabotshwa!* We do not mind being jailed! *Aluta Continua!* One people, one country! One trade, one trade union! An injury to one is an injury to all! Death to one is death to all! Freedom or death, the struggle is on, and victory is certain!

With freedom music in the air, will some of these boats ever make it to the harbor? Boat Kwandebele sank after hitting a freedom iceberg on December 11, 1986. Pretoria has since repaired it and is determined to sail it through the Blood Sea of resistance until it joins the other fleet of four at the Dead Sea.

The odds are great. Millions defiantly refuse to ride interminable reform boats. They hate being moved in never-ending merry-go-rounds—ever in transit. From township to Bantu location. From *tuisland* to homeland. From urban area to white area. From homeland prison to John Vorster Square. From Urban Council to Community Council. From baboon to kaffir. From aborigine to native. From African to Bantu. From cooperative to plural. From South Africans to Transkeians, Bophuthatswanans, Vendans, and Ciskeians. From citizens to "citizenship undetermined." From influx control to orderly urbanization. From singles to duals.

"Who are we?" people ask. "Yesterday we were citizens of here, today of over there, tomorrow citizens of in-between." From nonbeing to nonentity, worse than subhumans. Foxes have holes, birds have nests, and strangers have homes; but the sons and daughters of South Africa have no place to lay their heads. They refuse to sing with Jim Reeves: "This world is not my home, I am just passing through. My treasures are laid there, somewhere beyond the blue." But they are willing to pray with the persecuted former refugee: "I do not ask you to take them out of the world, but I do ask you to keep them safe from the evil one."

Apartheid river is in flood. It has been in flood for years, carrying down in its wrath many to Robben Island, Pollsmoor, and other countless prisons, police stations, and indoctrination camps. Before and after the macabre massacre of Sharpeville, many have been swept to death. Millions are suffocating and starving in homeland independence chambers. Adults and children have been detained (arrested and imprisoned without formal charges) in the tens of thousands.

The African freedom giant is on the march, from the shores to the interior, from the interior to the white beaches, from all four corners of the earth to the center, and from the center in all directions: into the cities, towns, townships, locations, primary schools, colleges, and universities. Into trade unions, churches, the press. Into individuals and groups. Into urban and rural areas. In the veins of every tribe flows the blood of unity. It flows against the white river of oppression and injustice, of exploitation and dehumanization. The odds are great. But many are willing to swim upstream, willing to swim in the River No:

- No to subhuman status;
- No to starvation in the land of plenty;
- No to landlessness when many farms lie fallow;
- No to perpetual boyhood and girlhood;
- No to indefinite slavery;
- No to nonstop floating;
- No to perpetual removals.
- No.

We shall sing,
Our children shall sing,
Our children's children shall sing,
As their grandparents did sing,
So will their grandchildren sing.

Permanent Tourists

April 6, 1652.
Dromedaris, *Reyger*, and *De Goede Hoop* docked at the Cape,
"Hundreds" marched out to bask in "our" sun.
A small garden in 1652,
An orchard halfway between East and West,
Said the Dutch East India Company.

It was night and it was day, the second phase.
Shout for joy, descendants of Shem!
Your gardens shall be your farms,
From orchards a country shall be born,
Another Holland at Africa's toe,
Said the Dutch East India Company.

And it was night and it was day, third stage.
Give way, descendants of Ham!
Your stock and land belong to our god,
Milk and honey not meant for you,
Unless you die, you'll draw our water and chop our wood,
Said the Dutch East India Company.

And it was night and it was day, the fourth stage.
Britannia rules the waves, Britannia rules the Cape!
Wake up, sons and daughters of Israel,
Leave Egypt in the great trek,
Free State, Transvaal, and Natal shall I give to you,
Said the prophet Piet Retief.

And it was night and it was day, the fifth phase.
Wake up, daughters and sons of Africa!
Two bulls for one knife no more,
Beggars cannot be choosers,
Guests do not accommodate their hosts,
Said the spirit of freedom!

And it was day and it was night, 1948.
Stand up, Broederbond! Wake up, Afrikaner giant!
The horse of power is here for you,
Jan Smuts shall walk, you take the saddle,
Gallop in the tested desert of divide-and-rule,
Said the united volk, nationalist powerbase.

And it was day and it was night, the darkest Sabbath.
Praise the Lord, Nederduits Gereformeerde Kerk!
Fast and feast, Hervormde Kerk!
Burn incense, Gereformeerde Kerk!
Sit on their backs, the White Sabbath is here,
Said the spirit of self-deceit.

The night came, the night went, Blacks' day.
Stand up, stand up, Bambata!
Shake off the yoke, Hintsa!
Tshaka and Sekhukhuni will take your side,
Makhado shall hold the north,
Said the voice of freedom.
Birth to Mandela!
Birth to Biko!
Birth to people's power!
Amandla!
Ngawethu!
United Democratic Nonracial Republic of South Africa.

I

TSHIUDA GROWS UP

1

Little Freedom Fighters

Little boys and girls. Some walked the whole way; some walked half the way. Others had to be carried on the back, the heads of their mothers already overburdened and overloaded by articles that had to be taken to the new government-designated resettlement area. They missed their mothers and fathers, who left before the cocks crowed and returned when the witches were on duty. The parents labored on the white man's farm, formerly their grandfather's land, or in the white man's hotel, built on their ancestors' sacred place. They labored day in and day out, three months a year for sweet nothing for their bitter sweat, nine months a year for one pound and two pounds, for women and men respectively. At times just a bag of cornmeal or kaffir mealie meal.

Little boys and girls. They were not allowed to visit their parents at work. Some did not, but many did. Against the law, and at a price. Some were beaten. Some were sentenced by the baas to farm labor on the spot. Parents were punished—at times physically in front of their children. At times their wages were cut in half. Little boys and little girls. They laughed and they cried. They ran. They promised never to do it again, and did it again. And again. And again.

They had no school and no church. They had no sports facilities. But they played. You saw them swimming, kicking at the water. Diving. Fathoming impossible depths and showing off all the styles. Untaught. They climbed trees and dangled, letting go to land on the ground far below. Even monkeys envied their skills in the games often reserved for apes. You watched them jumping and fighting and playing *tsingandedede,*[1] running in circles. They fished and hunted. They collected wild honey and caught birds and locusts. Forests provided fruits and vegetables that kept their health above average. Their teeth were firm and intact, and whiter than snow. Stronger than those of the dentist, who treated only whites' teeth along Krogh Street. Some were graduates from circumcision or initiation school. Some were undergraduates. Some were illiterate, called "clouds" by graduates.

Little boys and girls. Some were chosen to be nonnie's babysitter, to look after the white little girl. Some, like Mudzunga, who later became Sarah, and later Florah, looked after little white Hendrik and his younger brother Kallie. When they grew up, they beat her and kicked her, and when she gave them African medicine, a little spanking on the buttocks, she lost her fifty-pence-a-month job for nine months in a year. Her father, John, was told that she was lucky she was not shot. In fact, he was told that had he not been a good cook and chef at Clouds End Hotel, his daughter would have lost her life and he his well-paying job, five pounds a month for nine months in a year.

Little boys. They picked up cigarette stumps and smoked them until their fingers burned. Or they made their own tobacco rolls, which they hid when they came home. They picked up Coca-Cola and Sparletta bottles and sold them for a penny each to buy bread and sugar, the white man's miracle food.

Little boys. They saw a baas and his family living in a big tent under a *muumo* tree. He was one of the homeless poor whites. He begged for food from the black community. And he got it: pumpkins, sweet corn, sweet cane, green beans, cornmeal, chickens, *mabundu,*[2] and *halwa.*[3] Some of it Baas Mutetemelo, the

1. *tsingandedede:* a children's game of holding one another's hands, jumping in a circle, moving clockwise or counterclockwise.

2. *mabundu:* nutritional nonalcoholic corn drink.

3. *halwa:* traditional beer.

shivering baas (they did not have enough clothes for the winter cold), sold to whites driving past his makeshift home. When he had made enough money from the community's agricultural products, he started calling them names. The parents responded in idiomatic fashion:

Nyavhumbwa wa dagaila wa kanda vho u vhumbaho (Some people trample upon those who created them); *Tshinanaunga tshi tshi hula tshi u la thoho* (Some people you bring up and, when fully grown, they eat up your head); *Mutali u la kanwe, tsilu li la kanzhi* (A cunning person eats once, the fool eats many more times).

The little ones were different. They, like Mudzunga their sister, would fight back: the boys joined the monkeys to pick the mangoes, avocados, pears, peaches, oranges, and grapes that their parents had planted and nursed but could not eat. When the baas or the basies or the watchmen came, they disappeared into the thick bush, as agile and as fast as their fourlegged "kith and kin," so the baas thought. When they were forced to look after the cattle of the baas, they milked the cows into their mouths down into their bottomless little stomachs in the *veld* so that there was not enough for the calves and the slave drivers. Forced to plow, they stole the seed for their small hidden gardens in the river valley. When bulldozers carved open their ancestral graves to prepare the so-called Great North Road, they stoned them. They danced in muddied roads to make them impassable, and when cars got stuck, they got paid for pushing them out. Sometimes they smashed windshields of passing vehicles.

They were not always fortunate. One such victim drove past, and a few minutes later came back incognito. Milingoni and Tshiuda rushed to his car when he stopped, hoping to pick some pennies from his open hand. He grabbed both and beat them. Milingoni bit him and freed himself. Unfortunate Tshiuda, who was actually relieving himself under a bridge when Milingoni stoned the windshield, was left alone to face the baas's undeserved wrath. Standing among *minengeledzi*[4] trees, near Golf

4. *minengeledzi:* trees that grow on riverbanks.

Dam, safe beyond the reach of the baas, Milingoni shouted his advice to his captive brother: "*Li lume* (bite it)! *Li lume nga maanda* (bite it hard)! *Li lume kha madasi* (bite its genitals)! *Na nne ndo tou li luma la nnditsha* (I also bit it before it let me go)."

Little Tshiuda grabbed the baas by his privates. His wife and children shouted hell at the little baboon. Unrepentant, Tshiuda bit deep into the baas's arm—and deeper, and deeper—until the wife shouted: "*Ah! laat daai bobbejaan gaan* (let that baboon go); *hy maak jou seer* (he is hurting you). *Hy vreet aan jou vlees* (he is feeding on your flesh)." Baas threw his arm this way and that way, this way and that. But the baboon stuck, and bit deeper, crying the whole time. Baas found himself negotiating a ceasefire for the fight which he had started, which the baboons had provoked. In agony, he threw his hand this way and that way, up and down, cursing, pleading, begging, scolding, threatening to shoot with the gun he had left at home. Another swing saw Tshiuda flying and falling on his little back, rolling down the roadside. In a second he was up on his feet, looking straight into the baas's reddened face. "*Hardloop, bobbejaan, of ek gaan jou doodskop!* (run away, baboon, lest I kick you to death!)." Baas Incognito had clearly no desire to chase after his "escaped" prey, even less to continue the one-sided battle.

Now, among the other boys, bruised and swollen Milingoni and Tshiuda had become instant celebrities. A few boys laughed at them; but most envied their newly acquired experience and were full of questions: "What was it like, fighting Mukhuwa, the white provoker? Do his punches and kicks hurt? Are they hard or soft? Is it true that they are good at karate and boxing? Did you cry? What was he saying to you? But you bit him and beat him? His wife and children were afraid to come out of the car? Today you fought a white man. That's great! Perhaps one day we shall also get ours to fight—and bite." All Milingoni and Tshiuda, the new heroes, could do was feel their bruises and swellings, and joke between themselves: "I smell white. Did he leave some white paint on my face? Call me baas."

The news of the Golf Dam battle spread very fast, among

young and old: Milingoni and Tshiuda are the only men in the community! They bit and beat a white man. Up till now, only Mudzunga the babysitter had dared spank white boys. Their father was clearly shaken at the incident, fearing that police would come down on the whole family. Chief Liswoga was restless, anticipating police action against his tribe. The young boys were excited, knowing for the first time that harassing baas and his kith and kin was greater than "stealing" fruits and stoning cars. Whites can be bitten and beaten. In fact, young Makhaya from the Mabasha plantations, who was visiting at Thabeni, now told them that he had already beaten several white boys, some older than himself, bare-handed. He did not even need his sharp teeth. Parents, the chief, little boys and little girls—all knew, in spite of their fears, that baas can be beaten and forced to beg for mercy. Without a gun, baas is, after all, human all round. Man to man, he can be beaten; gun to gun, he can be defeated. Vhakoma, the chief's mother, started a new song:

Shonee kwangwa (We taught you a lesson)
Mukhuwa o kundwa wee (White is beaten)
Shonee kwangwa (We taught you a lesson)
Baas vho vhasa wee (Baas is burnt out)
Shonee kwangwa (We taught you a lesson)
Milingoni o linga wee (Milingoni did it)
Shonee kwangwa (We taught you a lesson)
Tshiuda tsho luma wee (Tshiuda bit him)
Shonee kwangwa (We taught you a lesson)
Madasi vho hoha wee (Genitals were pulled)
Shonee kwangwa (We taught you a lesson)
Vhasa lo tshema wee (Baas screamed)
Shonee kwangwa (We taught you a lesson)
Shango lashu li do vhuya wee (Our country shall come back)
Shonee kwangwa (We taught you a lesson)
Makhado[5] o vuwa (Great Makhado is resurrected)

5. Makhado: A great Venda chief who fought the Afrikaners in the mid-eighteenth century, winning some major victories.

Shonee kwangwa (We taught you a lesson)
Mavhuru o kundwa wee (Boers are defeated).

* * * * *

Swongozwi and Tshapinda, once living and lively communities, are no more. Destroyed. Between 1959 and 1965, the Thabeni community was uprooted. Once a flourishing maize- and bean-producing community, with able cattle farmers, it is gone. Annihilated. Mbabada, once a friendly, vivacious society, has disappeared. Madodonga is under a cloud of removal, as are perhaps both the Kutama and Sinthumule communities. Some people are under restrictions. Buried alive by the South African government. Apartheid, says Botha, is dead and outdated, but its stinking corpse is causing daily havoc among us. No, Botha is not in a hurry to bury it. Apartheid dead is more effective than apartheid alive.

Who am I, O God?

Persona Non Grata

Swongozwi, my fertile land,
Swongozwi, our great mountain!
  Tshapinda plains a fertile carpet at your feet:
  Your fields are life to our people,
  Your wild fruits health to our young!
Cursed 1951:
  By government decree,
  Authority without reason,
  Legislation without feeling,
  All blacks must move!
Will the powerful compensate the powerless?
  "Take your houses, if you can,
  Carry your fields' soil and water!"
The voice of power is the voice of truth,
The voice of government that of God!
  Bye, Swongozwi, my fertile land,

In white hands till freedom day,
Vox populi vox deo!
Epitaph:
We shall miss your fields,
Our orchards we shall see no more.
We shall miss your waters,
Our fruits we shall pick no more.
We shall miss your fauna and flora,
Our honey we shall eat no more.
We shall miss our history,
We shall miss our past.
We shall miss our roots,
We shall miss our graves.
We shall miss our dead,
We shall miss our baboons,
We shall miss our monkeys.
In white hands till freedom day,
Nkosi sikelel Afrika!
Thabeni, our gracious land,
Shall you comfort us to forget Swongozwi our fertile land?
Valleys and hills not so green,
Fields and rivers not so full of life,
What future have you in store for our young?
Cursed 1959:
By government decree,
Authority without reason,
Legislation without feeling,
All blacks must move!
Will the rich compensate the poor?
"Carry your souls if you can;
Take not your cattle, chickens, and goats!"
The voice of proclamation is the voice of good,
the voice of Pretoria is the voice of heaven!
Rest in peace, Thabeni, land of losses,
In white greed till the day of sharing,
The voice of sufferers is the voice of winners!

Epitaph:
We shall miss your cattle,
Our goats and chickens we shall see no more.
We shall miss your valleys and hills,
Our rivers we shall swim no more.
We shall miss your neighbors Tshifhawe and Tshilata,
Our traditional beer we shall drink no more.
We have lost our right to farm,
We have lost our right to eat.
We have lost access to water,
We have lost our right to drink.
Our dead shall miss the living,
Our living shall miss the dead.
Your birds shall miss our crops,
No bird meat for our young anymore.
In totalitarian hands till Uhuru day,
In the cry of the victim lives the seed of victory!
Mbabada, our new home of sand and stone,
How do you compare with Tshapinda, the land of plenty?
Flat land and thorn bushes everywhere,
Watermelons and kaffircorn not so good for me.
What's buried beneath these grey futureless sands?
Cursed 1961:
By government decree,
Authority without reason,
Legislation without feeling,
All blacks must be piled on top of one another!
Will the settled compensate the unsettled?
"Carry your hunger and thirst to the Promised Land,
The land of starvation and unmarked graves!"
The voice of continuous removals is the voice of order,
The label of impermanence our permanent status!
See you no more, Mbabada, cruel land,
May sandstorms sweep your valleys few and barren,
The voice in the desert is the dessert of hope!

Epitaph:
We shall miss our neighbors' milk,
Our melons and millet we shall relish no more.
We shall miss your thorns and sand dunes,
Our kids shall miss your polluted waters.
Venomous adder, poisonous scorpion, will you do without us?
We are tired of the beer of oppression,
We are tired of farming the rocks.
We are tired of hunger and thirst,
We are tired of burying our kith and kin.
We are tired of belonging nowhere.
Today citizens of here,
Tomorrow citizens of over there,
Next year citizens of in-between.
Scarecrows, nonentities that we are!
In perpetual motion till Mandela Day,
The voice of Pollsmoor, blueprint for the future!
Madodonga, land of hope and despair,
Mbabada, your distant cousin or twin sister?
Exposed to winds of wrath and drought of death,
Open to whirlwinds for years beyond the pale.
Any life beneath your sands and hope above the ground?
Cursed 1977:
By government decree,
By power without limit,
Legislation without mandate,
Consolidate Venda into one block!
Will the Boer empathize with the Bantu?
"Forsake your ideas and utopian dreams,
Enjoy your freedom in the Venda of plenty!
The mind of Pretoria knows what's good for you,
Amandla! Power! 1979 freedom year to serve the master!"
Shall we now leave our tamed desert?
Without wind and whirlwind, shall we survive?

The voice of defiance is our train to freedom,
Enough is enough, prison or freedom.
  We are here to stay, we are here to pray,
  We are here to pray, here to act!
  The voice of terror is not the voice of the shepherd!
Epitaph:
  We miss our fields,
  We miss our orchards.
  We miss our rivers,
  We miss our fruits.
  We miss our gardens,
  We miss our cattle.
  We miss our past,
  We miss our freedom, our being.
  Where is our humanity, Pretoria?
In suspension till Dagon's fall,
Minority power, usurper's power, majority voice that of
    government!
South Africa, my country black and beautiful,
South Africa, home for all black and white,
Citizenship for all that love and adore you,
Franchise for all men and women, mature and colorless.
My one undivided democratic nonracial South Africa!

2

Emerging Faith in Sinking Surroundings

By now the people's land had been confiscated and expropriated, to be given free or sold to poor Afrikaners at give-away prices. Below Hamathivhalifhade, Baas Gembral had now built a huge house. Above Hatshavhuyo, Baas Oom Kierie was busy putting up a mansion on the table-like mountaintop. At Tshamathiyana, Scot McGregor (or as the local people knew him, Tshikotshi Magiriki) had first put up caravan park and later his orchard and then his garden and then his winter house and also his horse stable and a big kraal for his cattle. Malimuwa, Lukheli, and Hafunyufunyu had been taken, divided, and shared among Afrikaners several years before.

The local people had become farmhands, their fields reduced or taken away altogether, their stocks culled for causing soil erosion. Or, as was the case with old Masotsha, some lost their stock to the baas, because every goat, every cow, and every fowl that trespassed into the baas's territory automatically became his property. It was in this way, old one-armed Langwane asserted, that Baas Gumutsha (hornless baas) had become a rich poultry farmer. When he first came here, he used to beg for eggs for Nonnie Rita and Basie Pieter. Within two years the local people had lost almost all their chickens to him, and he was selling hundreds every day.

"Look at Baas Tshivhalamadana," the people said, "the one who counts cash in hundreds. When he came here, did we not feed him and his family on goat's milk and *tshidzimba?*[1] Today

1. *tshidzimba:* simple maize grains mixed with beans.

when you go to the vendusie, where they sell their cattle, you see *tshivhalazwigidi,* the one who counts his money in thousands, and *tshivhalamakhulo,* the one who counts his money in millions, taking their money to the bank in wheelbarrows. Where are our cattle? All taken. Where are our fields? All taken. What are our wages? A few penny coins thrown at us two weeks after the month's end! We must run like little chickens picking at *mufhoho*[2] grains.

What is soil erosion? Rubbish. Nonsense. White lies. Witchcraft. In our hands, our cattle cause erosion—erosion—erosion! In their hands, our cattle mean money—money—money! Meat for their children! When their cattle multiply, it is a sign of good farming skills. They get more land, more subsidies, more veterinarians, more everything. When ours multiply, we are irresponsible—guilty of overgrazing the land. Can cattle and goats and sheep graze on my palm? Everything is gone. Maneledzi is now Williespoort. Lushi is Punchbowl. Malimuwa is Mountain Inn. Swongozwi is Hanglip. *Tshitandani-tsha-ha-nyatsisa-nwana-u-bebe-pholisa*[3] is now Louis Trichardt. Our chief and his *vhatanuni,* his royal wives, are now farmhands. *Nthu anga khea:*[4] here is my spittle on the ground; this will not go too far."

* * * * *

At faraway Lushi, one good farmer and his neighbors put up a small school for black children. The one unqualified teacher continually had her hands full with problems from farmers who would not let their herdboys or babysitters waste time with a, e, i, o, u. A few parents feared that too much education would corrupt their boys. On his return from a five-year diamond mine stint in Kimberley, Masindi had withdrawn his two sons from a Catholic school some eighty miles away. As he put it, he would

2. *mufhoho:* corn-type grain, with a head like a clenched fist.

3. Sarcastic praise-song meaning, "Drop your baby and carry police on your back."

4. Making an oath, swearing that something will surely happen.

not let his children become what he saw in Khimbini, the diamond city, where young men would walk along talking to books or to themselves, mumbling things that only the mentally deranged are capable of. Some had become arrogant and disrespectful toward their parents. Some even dumped their religion in favor of something called Craftianity. They accepted a white god. Have they become white? It is madness. *Thoho i a lwa na mutsinga?* (Does the head fight the neck?) Or the tree its roots? He had seen beautiful girls lose value in the marriage market. Who would marry a girl who never kneels? A girl who cannot smear cow dung in the hut or courtyard? A girl who cannot carry a water pot unsupported on her head? No. No one would pay bride cattle for a girl who wears short pants like a man. Two bulls in one kraal?

Tshifhenya and Mudzusi have a different opinion. They have long smuggled their boys out to stay with friends at faraway places where they can learn to read and write. They will not let white farmers lay hands on their children—their boys. It did not take long for other families to follow suit. Within a few years, farmers openly encouraged their boys and girls, black men and women, to try harder to produce more boys than girls for farm labor. As more boys simply disappeared, and later also a few girls, the farm labor shortage reached a crisis point.

Young men like Magaga and Petrus and Marandela had left for Johannesburg and other cities long before. When they came home at Christmas, it was kept a secret. The farmers never knew, for after all, were not Milandu and Mutshinyalo, the chief's sons, among the *magaraba,* those who came home once a year at Christmastime? When the *magaraba* departed again, they left behind gramophones and music discs, or "music plates," as these were known among the people. Rural music started to mix with urban music, *malende*[5] side by side with jive, *tshigombela*[6] side by side with dance, *mbila*[7] side by side with guitar. Here one thing was sinking into the

5. *malende:* traditional music and dance.
6. *tshigombela:* traditional music and dance.
7. *mbila:* traditional musical instrument.

ground, here one thing into another; here things were falling apart, here things were marrying. Some things had gone away with the land, but landlessness had brought new things in its advance.

* * * * *

The local *nanga*[8] had been baptized some thirty years back, something quite rare among traditional doctors. Perhaps his long stay in the golden city Egoli, his years of night school, his time as a farmer and now his new role as chief cook and chef had brought a flexibility of character unusual among his own species. But he no longer goes to church. He rarely reads his Bible, and he does not encourage his family to go to church. His ancestors are probably happier with him now than is the white man's god, with whom he apparently had a flirting affair. He enjoyed his beer once in a while, but nobody remembers seeing him drunk. He was an avid storyteller around a winter evening fire, and his children loved and admired him; but this familiarity never bred contempt. There was always a closeness between father and children, but also a mythical distance, almost a gulf unbridgeable. One of his sons admired his physique, his way of walking, his way of dress, the way he ate and chewed, even his way of drinking. "Watch him walk behind the plow! Watch him cut the trees! Look at him collecting honey!" When he rebuked, he did it one at a time, never mixing and mincing his tongue and gums and teeth, never repeating himself. He always coined his own word to avoid an obscene word. *Ntshimba yau,* instead of *matshimba au,* was his euphimistic way of saying "your shit."

When Tshiuda, one of his sons, brought him birds, he was quick to say, "*Ahee mudau,*[9] roast them; bring three for me and share seven with your sisters and brothers. Perhaps your great mother, your mother, and your younger mother will also need some." Within a few minutes, the young lion, the *mudau,* would have the *magwede* and *thonzhe* birds roasted and ready.

8. *nanga:* medicine man, doctor.

9. *Ahee mudau:* thank you, lion (the lion was his totem animal).

* * * * *

At Booysen's, one Zionist[10] prophet set up his church. He became its bishop and his wife, the *vhakhokheli*, its spiritual mother. It became known that he preached, taught, and healed. He also spoke in heavenly languages. Musandiwa, Tshiuda's mother, had been ill for several years already, since the birth of her last born, Tshimangadzo, the surprise who came less than a year and a half after the birth of her elder sister Mushaisano. Ratshilumela, her doctor husband, had tried every medicine and every ritual, including the malombo dance, but the ancestors would not listen—which did no little harm to his standing as the great *nanga*. He even let her go to hospital on different occasions. And he easily let her go when she requested to visit the Zionist prophet.

But on her return she vowed never to go back again. Why, she boiled, did he lay hands on her breasts? The pain, she had told him, was in her legs and arms and stomach—not in her breasts. It had not been until after she was married that she allowed Ratshilumela to touch her breasts. She drinks, perhaps at times a little too much; but nobody has ever dared touch her breasts. Why should this little prophet, yesterday's child, touch her breasts? "He takes only a few minutes to pray for twenty men, jumping from one to the other, hardly touching their heads. With women he kneels down, he crawls, he crouches, he roars, he foams, he trembles, his mouth waters like a lion that has caught prey—and then he clings to your breasts. Like Tshimangadzo, my little daughter. If he had done this to me some twenty years ago, I, Musandiwa, would have broken his neck. Ask your father what I did to one hefty man who attempted to 'sleep me' when I was collecting wood at Swongozwi. When your father arrived to finish him off, I had already done half the job: he was no longer a man good for anything. I had brought down all his *vhugala*—

10. Zionist: here a member of an independent African church, the Church of Mt. Zion.

all his glories. *Nne musandiwa, hu tshee kale hu tshee mulovha, mutamvu u tshee na thodzi* (That was I, Musandiwa, yesterday, some time ago, when I was still a *mutamvu* tree with a sharp top branch)."

Makhadzi, the chief's sister, lived behind the mountain, at the foot of a hill. She sold *Mbamba* beer for a living and prayed at faraway Gertrudsburg mission station for eternal life. Her integrity and audacity convinced Musandiwa to travel with her one Sunday for worship. While in church, after a ten-mile walk, Musandiwa listened to every word and watched every move by the local pastor. When the first service was over and children were sent away and the curtains were drawn for the celebration of *tshilalelo,*[11] Musandiwa wondered what this evening meal at midday would be all about. Why chase away other people? Whose body in the dish and whose blood in the cup? Human blood and flesh for food? The pastor came to her, said a prayer and made a cross sign on her forehead, and asked her to leave and wait in his house. Her son went with her.

On the way home she had more questions raised than answered: "Why did some men go while their wives stayed behind? Why did people go in one by one to a small room at the back of the church? Why do people pay money in the church? Who takes it?" She was very satisfied with the way the pastor dressed: long black dress and something on the neck that made him look like a female crow. He walked properly. He spoke well, with love and respect, although she did not understand much of what he said. There was no jumping about and making eyes at women. Men sat by themselves. Women by themselves. Boys by themselves. Girls by themselves. Children with their mothers. Everything had *tshirunzi,*[12] dignified all the way.

Last, and most important, pastor Necodemus Masekela and his wife Margaret are cool and human beings. Their eyes do not tell stories. Musandiwa knows crooks when she sees them. Above

11. *tshilalelo:* holy communion.
12. *tshirunzi:* dignity.

all, she loved the prayer, the manner of it rather than the content, which she could hardly understand. She also needed an explanation for the sign: "He cut me down and cut me across the face, cutting down my pains. He must be a great *nanga,* but I did not see his medicine!"

At home around the evening fire, Musandiwa related her day's experience. All were captivated. Gone were the laughter and mockery that followed the Booysen's experience: "Did we not tell you not to go? Today you met the white god, didn't you? He likes breasts and he roars, doesn't he? Did the prophet tell you who bewitched you? Come ma, you are healed today. Come, pray! Did you see wonders at Zion as they sing, 'Zion Vhona madembe,' from Friday night through Sunday evening? If you had not left on time, today you would be the bishop's wife!" By the end of the year Musandiwa knew most of the book of laws, the *katekisima.* She sang one hymn after another, teaching them to her children and herself.

Rumors were circulating that the black township of Tshikota, or Masagani, the place of bags, would be demolished for it was too old and unclean. So would Gertrudsburg. So would Thabeni. Privately, in the communities, people whispered: "Whites do not want us too close to them. They also want to give fertile Gertrudsburg to white farmers." One missionary and one black teacher whispered too loudly and got visits from the security police. At Thabeni all black farmers had to cut their stock to four head of cattle per family or leave. When they chose to leave, they were forbidden to take their stock with them, for this would "spread disease." Some sold to butchers, others to white farmers, at give-away prices. Everything was still sinking around them: the land, the stock, the religion, the health, the price, the culture, life as they knew it.

What is happening with this government?

Public Enemy Number One

If it were only an ugly word,
If we were dealing with a policy gone astray,
Or an ideology among others;
I would call professors together,
I would gather sociologists;
Anthropologists would explain the culture
In a classroom or five-star hotel.
Then we would learn and unlearn the past;
We would know what makes apartheid tick;
We would know the seed of greed.
We would know the secret of self-inflicted fear
That enslaves freedom fighters of old,
Seated now on their neighbor's back.
   It is a religion: god in Satan's hand!

If it were only an election slogan,
If we were faced with ordinary human disease,
Or a temptation amongst ten;
I would appeal to Moses of old;
I would invite the wise from east and west;
From the north and south solutions would come,
As wise and fools mix fortunes in the same pot.
Then we would discover what reform will do,
That enriching the rich will not impoverish the poor,
That polishing the corpse of an apartheid shoe
Would give birth to a democratic boot.
Crushing the thorns that prick the soul;
Raising Lazarus from among the dead;
Giving hope to Martha and Mary.
   It is cancer.

If it were only Afrikaners behind the wheel;
If other whites would be like stainless steel,
Or at least neutral between wolf and flock;

I would appeal to conscience and science.
I would tap on English tradition.
French Revolution would be no proper dose;
Talk to talk and not eye for an eye;
As we belabor from dawn to dusk,
All our needs and deeds of the past,
And find solutions before the gale,
Avoiding pains in the groin.
This patient is unlike others:
Like Hitler on the white horse,
Galloping down the precipice.

3

Survival and Progress on a Diet of Poison

Only a few families remained at Thabeni. Some went to Tshikuwi, some to Dzanani, some to Sinthumule, some to other farms. Some to nobody knows where. Others, like Ratshilumela and Musandiwa and their family, to Kutama. Chief Kutama gave them land to build on and farm at Mbabada, one of his many villages.

This is a dry land of sand and thorn shrubs good for sorghum and watermelon and *gwadi,* a pumpkin-like vegetable. In good rainy years, maize, sweet cane, groundnuts, and beans do well. Perhaps once every ten years—or more. Or less. Except for the fertile valleys along the Soutparsberg mountains, now almost all in white hands, there is very little fruit to speak of here: bitter *matshili,* sour *rabure,* bitter *namana,* sweet *thedwa. Mafula* is used for *mukumbi* beer, while the seed is crushed for its nuts or *thebvu;* but as a fruit it has been reputed to cause heavy flu or "fruit malaria"—*dali* in the local language. For Vhongwaniwapo, the aboriginal citizens, this flat sandy land is their paradise, although they still bemoan the loss of Eden below the mountains. For those not among the Ntangiwakugalas, the first to occupy this land, for the Ratshilumelas from Swongozwi, this is a windy cursed desert where the kaffircorn or sorghum is as tasteless as the sandy soil.

Almost thirty years ago, this country of more than seven villages had only one school, from grade one to standard six, or grade eight.[1] All who were taught here were pupils, or school

1. In South Africa, primary school consisted of grades 1 and 2, then standards 1 through 6.

children; students were those at secondary, or high school. Only they studied. At primary school the pupils had to listen, cram, and reproduce. They could ask who, what, and when; they had to be cautious about the hows and the whys. Why, for example, did they sit on stones in grades one through five? Why did some of them learn under a tree, or just out in the open, or in classrooms made of wood planks with roofs falling apart? Why did they have to buy their books, pencils, and crayons while they also paid school fees and sports fees? Why were they sent home if they could not afford these fees? Why were most of their teachers unqualified, called private teachers? Why did they have to run many miles every day to and from school, in winter, in the rain, in the hot sun? How was it possible that white children in Louis Trichardt and on neighboring farms had everything free from the government, while poverty-stricken black parents had to pay for everything?

Many children knew about these disparities. They discussed them among themselves, and found answers for themselves. But not Tshikindi. Having just come back from Mamelodi in Pretoria, where he attended grades one to three, he asked Piet the teacher why the government did not provide chairs or benches. Private teacher Piet had a simple answer: such questions belong to standard four. In standard six Tshiuda asked the same question in the class. Qualified teacher Francis asked him if he wanted to join a Nelson Mandela in the Rivonia trial.

After school, Tshiunda visited Francis in his two-room mud house to follow up on his question and get an explanation of the Rivonia Mandela. Francis was a good teacher, a very able teacher. He was strict but loving, truthful but cautious—too cautious. A devout Catholic, he pulled Tshiuda outside, touched his finger on his forehead, chest, and shoulders in a cross sign. "Look, my son," he said, "your questions are good but dangerous. Dangerous for you and for me. You see, many, many schools used to belong to the church. Almost all are in the hands of the government today. Black and white used to go to school together, not everywhere, but in many places. We learned the same things, and many blacks did better than whites. It is now different. The syllabus is different. To tell you the truth, Bantu education—I mean education for black people—is poison.

"When I compare your books with our books, your syllabus with our syllabus, I often cry. If you knew what I get and what a white teacher gets per month, you would cry. Look, I must stay here for the whole week and bicycle home every Friday to come back on Sunday night. I cannot afford to go back and forth by bus every day. Mandela and his people are now on trial for saying what I am saying, for fighting these things. My boy, you have a future. We promoted you from grade two to standard one, and from standard two to four. In my class you are doing very well. Learn. Cram. Reproduce. Keep your mouth tightly closed.

"Our people say, '*Vhandalala fuvhuvhu u do la vhufa ha tombo*' (you lie waiting patiently along a stone, and you will be its heir). I trust you. If you tell anybody what I told you, I will lose my job and be arrested. You too. Fortunately, we know how to handle this poison so that it does not kill you. We shall make you men and women in spite of it. God is not a child. Now go."

Tshiuda hesitated and opened his mouth, but Francis cut him short: "Go! Go away! This is time for tree planting. You cheated me last Friday by pushing into the ground a rootless branch of a *muserenga* tree. I gave you an egg[2] for that. You will get another nought this week."

Principal Kwaho arrived unexpectedly. "Good afternoon, Principal. This boy is becoming naughty these days. He came late for music practice this morning, and now he is asking grammar questions during a tree-planting period—after school!"

Their good teacher loved eggs and told them so. He even asked for them. One morning he came in fuming, for in the eggs that Mdungazi had brought him a day before, he found two fully grown little owls. He stopped them from bringing him more eggs, but Mdungazi still scored good marks. A week later Dyela did not come to school. Some standard six boys were sent to fetch

2. egg: zero.

him. When Francis told him to ride the horse, the high bench on which he would get four lashes on his behind, Dyela brought forward extenuating circumstances: "I do not do well in the class. You taught us, sir, that fish helps to build the brain. I was fishing all these days. Today they found me at Litshovhu River. I had three *ndungula* fishes and one *tshikwea.*" They all burst into laughter, including the teacher himself, as Dyela jumped off the horse to his freedom and the teacher threw his stick out the window.

In standard six, Madiabatho told visiting inspector White that he wanted to become a pilot. Jericho wanted to be a train driver; Mhlamali wanted to be a journalist, while Mangata wanted to become a lawyer. Mr. White called "Scotch," their teacher, into the principal's office. The students could hear a heated argument raging in the office. When Mr. White came back, he told the class to stop daydreaming. When he moved to the next class, "Scotch" twisted his lips in defiance, saying, "I am Scotch and I'll never die. I will kick him out through that wall. You do what I tell you. He can tell his nonsense to his wife, not me. From today you Tshiuda, you Mhlamali, and you Jericho are in standard six. Your promotion has been accepted. Work hard. I want first classes from you. You Satan, *Muswane wau.*[3] Shall we all be teachers and nurses and clerks and drivers and laborers? I want my boys to fly in the air! To be judges and magistrates! To be journalists and lawyers and doctors! Why should we keep on extinguishing the fires of aspirations among our people? Smothering their hopes? Go to hell, Satan! *Muswane wau.*"

As for you, black one, what are the prospects?

* * * * *

They went to school together. They came home together. They would walk, and they would run. Some would go two or three on one bicycle. Almost all without shoes. Some brought porridge with them, all makes: *vhutete, mutuku, tshisese, mufumbu, phuthu,*

3. Euphemism for "your shit . . ."

with vegetables, meat, fish, eggs, or just salt, which they mixed with water to make a cock, or rather cockdrink, euphemism for nothing. From a few well-to-do families came boys and girls with bread and biscuits and cookies and sweets. Occasionally some of them bought quarter loaves for a tickey each, which they shared among two, four, six, even ten hungry souls. The poorest of the poor rushed to the nearby *rabure* and *namana* trees during break to compete with the *doliana* and *dzwiavhavha* birds for the available bitter fruits. The birds would often leave enough behind, at more accessible branches, as if they understood the plight of Maligana and George, who had long lost their fathers. Even the *rabure* on the ground, in the dust, ended up in someone's stomach.

They did not know how. They did not learn later. They may never know in the future. But one day they saw people cooking soft porridge and some sort of gravy between the old and new sections of their school. During break, the principal announced that all pupils could line up for food. They used cupped hands. And leaves. And papers. And every container they could lay their hands on. They drank the gravy and swallowed the porridge. School prefects and stronger boys and their girlfriends got the delicious and nutritious bran-like crispies, popularly called *tshigume.* The gravy did not taste good at first but after a week even their teachers would eat both the gravy and *tshigume* with their bread. Some stole the gravy powder, and now and again the *tshigume* dust would fall out of someone's pocket. Others, like Tshiuda, took gravy home in bottles. In class, Marandela and Annah, among others, would no longer fall asleep or wander away from lessons in a pensive mood, wondering what they would eat the next day. Now they had only to worry about dress and their unfortunate brothers and sisters at home. Even for these, they could still steal and hide something in their pockets and book cases.

One morning Inspector White came with two black supervisors, his juniors. At the end of the morning prayer session, Inspector White announced that they all looked healthy and would no longer need the *kupugani* soup. The drought was also broken, he added. Back to square one. They walked and ran and cycled on their dusty roads and footpaths to and from school, feeding on the dust of the land and the dust of Bantu education. They saw the food come, and they saw it go. Like smoke.

In town they saw the double-story white schools. They saw their school buses and their beautiful uniforms. They saw them eating well-balanced foods and drinking milk. In good and in bad years. In times of drought and in times of plenty. At street junctions they saw special people appointed in the morning and in the afternoon to control the traffic lest one precious white child be run over and the number of the already "endangered species" be reduced. They saw. They wondered. They debated from within. They acquiesced. Reluctantly.

Government Gone Crazy

There was once a Saul chosen of God:
  Born of the small tribe of Benjamin,
  Small tribe, humble beginnings.
Elevated by the hand of God:
  Seated on the throne of power,
  A king among kings,
  To lead and serve his nation Israel;
  To rule in justice and in love,
  To care for the orphan and the widow,
  To offer shelter to the stranger,
Above all to serve the king of kings, Yahweh the Kingmaker.

There was once a Lucifer chosen of God:
  Full of self, drunk with pride,
  Futile coup against God he led.
Misled by thirst for power:
  He drew his sword against the Almighty,
  An evil angel among his evil crowd,
  To lead a revolt against the Ancient of Days:
  To promote evil against good,

To establish injustice, not righteousness,
To deny food to the hungry and water to the thirsty,
And above all to rob God of his godly rights.

In 1948 a government was born:
Born of the Voortrekker tribe,
Of Dutch descent, of French Huguenots.
Elevated by the barrel of the gun:
Entered into covenant with the god of self,
A bloodthirsty god, god of Blood River;
In God's name to maim and kill,
In his name to rob and misrule,
To crush the soulless black kaffir race,
To hewing wood and drawing water;
Above all to serve Shem and Japheth, the white tribe.

Strange twins, apartheid and reform:
Born of barren parents, bankruptcy of mind,
Public Safety Act—insecurity for public at large.
1967 Terrorism Act—terror for all,
1982 Internal Security Act—turmoil for all.
Ever heard laws sing like a choir?
Rock 'n' roll apartheid music of oppression:
Legislate against blackness,
Detain and torture young and old.
Security's call: maim and kill,
Kill black ideas, hopes and dreams,
Above all, their desire to be like God and us.

State of emergency 1960, born of fear:
State of emergency 1985,
State of emergency 1986,
1987 Urgent State of Emergency.
Ever heard the voice of truth?
Gospel music of South African Broadcasting Corporation:
All are happy save communists,

All secure everywhere,
Situation under control,
Peace reigns countrywide,
Above all, white man, you are in control.

Take off your hats, honor the great patriot,
Johan Coetzee, greatest of police commissioners,
His mouthpiece the government gazette:
Law and Order, Baal and Asherah,
Campaign not for your beloved ones,
No projects to set them free:
Freedom's not good for them,
Worship Internal Security Act 1982,
Shout not, call not for their release,
Above all, take to heart Romans Thirteen.

Not by telegram, pen and ink!
Disapprove not detention without trial,
Not by document, not by protest, pen and ink!
Freedom-poster, sticker, and T-shirt all taboo,
Think not, speak not, act not, feel not.
Protest gatherings not for you:
Disgraced by government, dishonored by you,
Wisdom menu June 12, '86,
Security garment December 11, '86,
April 10, '87 washdown,
Above all, glory to God, from whom all governments come.

4

Education at High and Low Places

There were good times in the valley. At Mphephu Secondary School students came from all over the northern Transvaal. Some stayed in dormitories, others with friends and relatives. They spoke Venda, Sotho, Shangaan, and a few other languages. There were fights among rural and urban students, at times over nothing, at times over girls, at times over stolen books, at times just because it was the right age for fights. A few students fought their teachers, but only when student and teacher interests converged on one member of the opposite sex. These incidents were few and far between.

The teachers were good; very good. Good in almost everything. In science. In music. In sports. In all the subjects. The pass rate was high, and the facilities were reasonable.

Tshiuda stayed with his *nanga* grandmother. His father's intention was that he would learn African traditional medicine as well as Western medicine. By the time he completed high school, he would have learned much from Tsanwani, his grandmother at Madzhatsha, a village in the valley. But before he could commit himself to African medicine, he tested the old lady's skills, particularly her divining skills.

There were two huts. Grandson and grandmother shared the kitchen hut. At night, Tshiuda threw clay clods at the inside of the roof and let them fall on the fire place, then hid under his blankets. Granny would wake up and wake her already snoring grandson. After several repetitions, the old lady and Dubulasi, her son, became very concerned. Neither realized that the clods had been hidden under Tshiuda's blanket. "Why should Granny not take up the divining bones to smell out the culprit?" Tshiuda suggested. In no time the bones were poured out of the skin bag, the *thevhele.* She picked them up and threw them up and down a few times in her hands, occasionally blowing into them. She said: "Tell us. Tell us, you who know. See for us. See for us, you who have eyes. You have ears. Hear for us, you who do not sleep. Why shall your grandson not enjoy his sleep? And I, a sick old lady? Tell us. Tell us, you who know. Who is behind this? Who is behind us? Tell us, you who know."

She threw the bones out on the floor. Pushed one that way. Pulled one this way. Turned some to face her son. Some to face her. And when she turned one with six eyes to face Tshiuda, he almost passed out. She arranged and rearranged them, murmuring in between, "No, they shall speak. No, they shall tell. They are telling lies; they shall tell the truth. If they do not, I shall burn them. No, I am not going to give them rest till they put my mind to rest. The witch is not far away. Perhaps a member of the family. [This scared Tshiuda to the marrow—momentarily, until she proceeded.] If it is my daughter-in-law, tell me, you who know."

Her hefty son, Dubulasi, wondered whether he should not wake his wife, since one bone was facing the hut where she slept. "Not yet," said the mother. "You throw them up, Dubulasi. Tell them to tell us the truth. You are doing well. Again! Blow into them. Again. Give them to Tshiuda." By now, Tshiuda had been a baptized Christian for almost a year, since December 15, 1963, to be exact. "I am a Christian, I can't handle *thangu,* these divining bones. I am sorry, but I cannot." Dubulasi rose in fury: "Witches will come in through you. The other day you refused to be sprinkled with treated water. You are a dangerous opening in this family. I am going to send you back to your father. You think we are mad? We are your parents. Is she not your grandmother? Do you think your father does not know what he is doing by sending you here?"

Dubulasi's mother calmed him down. "After all, Tshiuda is a little boy. He will learn. *Thangu* have already exposed the culprit.

It was not even necessary for Tshiuda to handle them. *Thangu* have caught the knee.[1] The culprit is one of us. Our neighbor. This Shangaan wife of my own grandson is trying to kill me and Tshiuda, my grandson. I die for my *mundende*, my old-age pension. He dies for his education. You, my son, may be next. But before I am too sure, I will consult the cave *mungome*, the diviner who lives in the cave, tomorrow. You know all too well our saying, No doctor treats himself.[2] For tonight I will hold the wolves at bay. They won't come again. If they do, I will send them back to chew her who sent them."

But before they slept again, Tshiuda asked for permission to put out the fire so that the witches would not easily see them again. The old lady agreed, not knowing that, besides testing her divining skills, the clod incidents were aimed at forcing her to agree to extinguish the fire every night. The fire was making the hut unbearably hot, encouraging the bedbugs out of their hiding places to feast, mostly on the tender steak of her young grandson. For grandma Tsanwani, there was only one season in a year—winter.

1. Smelled out a member of the family.
2. *Mudengu ha didenguli.*

5

Labor Machines, Tongues, and Baboons

[The year is 1965, January through May, in Louis Trichardt.]

White Tom: Ten kitchen and garden boys! [he shouted from behind the counter of the labor distribution office, situated just below the imposing Dutch Reformed Church, reportedly built in honor of the god who blessed the Boers' guns and cannons that neutralized the fierce resistance of Khosi Makhado,[1] the Lion of the North, in the nineteenth century].

Black Tom: [translating the baas and as always adding spice and salt] The baas needs healthy, able-bodied boys. Not some of you incapacitated by *mbamba*[2] and old women.

* * * * *

To the white community, White Tom was a godsend, an expert on all Bantu matters; he kept the Bantu in his place. He "knew" three Bantu languages: Venda, Sotho, and Shangaan. The blacks knew better. The expert had only a faltering knowledge of Venda, not what one would call working Venda. His vocabulary consisted mostly of curse words and imperatives that would come in bursts and spurts, belching and burping with punctuations of "kaffir," "baboon," "donder" (thunder), "domkop" (fool), and many more unprintable expletives.

The labor office was a busy place, operating five days a week. Usually twice a day, black boys and girls, aged anywhere between

1. King Makhado: head of the Venda tribe in the nineteenth century.
2. *mbamba:* home-brewed beer with a high alcohol content.

usability and the grave, would crowd in as the Tom twins, themselves opposite racial poles, scream-shouted jobs into the air in Afrikaans and Venda: "*Twaalf kaffertjies vir nagwerk!*[3] *Kafuri dza fumi na mbili dza u hwala mibvelangannda!*" (twelve little kaffirs for toilet and night soil work). "*Vyf kaffermeid vir huiswerk, was, nonnies en basies, op te pas en kook!*" "*Kafuri thanu dza vhasidzana dza u shuma nduni, u kuvha na u lela vhononi na vhovhasi!*" (five kaffir maids for domestic service, laundry, baby-sitting small baases and nonnies, and cooking). "Boys for Sheefeera Timber Works. Farm boys. Hotel girls. Loading boys. Packaging girls. Mine boys. Factory boys. Town park boys. Game park boys. Stay-in girls. Sleep-out maids."

All boys and all girls, no matter what their age. No men and no women. Forever children. Five days a week. Once or twice a day. Or thrice a week. Without prior warning. Everything was left to the forces of supply and demand, of demand and supply, of fate and whim. They would fall over one another, head over heels, helter-skelter, throwing their passes and *spentshelas*[4] into a big heap before the two benefactors, pleading: "Mine, please mine, Baas. I have come for two weeks now . . . two months . . . six months. . . . I work hard, Baas. Baas can ask this one . . . any job, Baas . . . for anything, Baas. . . ." There were many heart-breaks and tears—and a few celebrations.

Tshiuda was lucky on his first attempt. Armed with an endorsed special pass from Chief Kutama, he landed a job on the first day. From the labor office, he walked the one mile to 133 Kruger Street and handed his workpapers to the housewife, the Mevrou. "*Staan daar by die deur* (wait there at the door)," she said and called her husband, the Meneer.

"Do you speak good kafferkaans?"[5] asked the Meneer.

Tshiuda nodded in bewilderment.

"I speak good Afrikaans, Meneer . . . sir."

3. *nagwerk:* Tshikota black township used the hated bucket system for toilets.

4. *spentshelas:* a special pass given to boys and girls under sixteen.

5. kafferkaans: Kaffer Afrikaans, Afrikaans spoken by blacks.

The Meneer and Mevrou looked at each other, told him to "staan daar," and walked around the garage to the *kafferhok*,[6] the servants' quarters. The husband had an oxhide whip, called *sjambok* in Afrikaans. Next Tshiuda heard the crackling of the *sjambok*, a short-lived struggle, and a black man of about eighteen shot past him like a bullet from the Makhulumasindi, the feared Boer cannon machinegun that drove away Khosi Makhado some hundred years before. He disappeared into nowhere. Nonnie and basie, their four- and six-year-old daughter and son, appendaged their approval: "He was a cheeky kaffirboy. Bad boy, wasn't he?"

Riding on the wave of his newfound confidence, the baas turned to Tshiuda and said, in Afrikaans, "What is your name?"

"Simon, Meneer."

"Where is your home, boy?"

"Madodonga, Meneer."

"What is your headman's name, boy?"

"Madodonga, Meneer."

"What are your father's and mother's names?"

"Ratshilumela and Musandiwa, Meneer."

"Do they work, boy?"

"Yes, Meneer."

"For which baas?"

"For themselves, Meneer."

"What do they do?"

"My father has a small garden. A small field. He is also a *nanga*—a doctor—works with medicine. My mother is a housewife."

"Boy, is that work? A *toordokter*—witchdoctor? He does not work for white people, he has no baas?"

"He works, Meneer. He had an orchard. And a big garden. Before that he worked in Johannesburg. He had a hundred and forty head of cattle, Meneer. He lost everything, Meneer. He is now old, Meneer. He works for himself, Meneer."

"Was your father ever arrested for anything?"

6. *kafferhok:* literally, the "kaffir fowl run."

"I do not know, Meneer. Perhaps only for a pass, Meneer.[7] And for somebody who tried to assault my mother, Meneer."

"How many brothers and sisters have you?"

"Nine sisters and seven brothers, Meneer."

"From one female? Oh boy!"

"No, Meneer. My father has three wives, Meneer."

"*Jeslaaik!* My Jesus! Th-th-ree w-wives!?"

"Y-y-yes, Meneer."

"Some of them are half-sisters and half-brothers?"

"No. Nobody is half anything. I have an elder mother, my mother, and my younger mother—*mmemuhulu, mmeanga na mmane wanga.* I have three mothers, nine sisters, and seven brothers. Full mothers. Full brothers. Full sisters. Full father. All of us are lions—*vhadau!*"

"And you have one father?"

"I said so."

"His name?"

"Ratshilumela."

"The special pass says 'John'?"

"That is his white name, Meneer."

"Is he a Christian?"

"Yes."

"Which church?"

"Used to be Zion, now he does not go."

"Toordokter Christian? Name of the Baptist on a toordokter?"

"He was baptized in the African Church of Zion, Meneer. He has many Bibles: English, Afrikaans, Shona, Venda, Sotho, Zulu, Tsonga. He says he prays, Meneer. He is not an evil man. God helps him help other people, he says. To heal them. To protect them against evil and evildoers. He fights off lightning strikes. Protects crops against insects. To break the drought. He helps childless couples. Ancestors help him locate and prepare effec-

7. Being arrested for a pass violation was considered a respectable offense. No black man was truly a man unless he landed behind bars several times in a year for a pass offense.

tive medication. Mad people are brought to him. He says he does not work against God."

"Toordokter helping people? Working with God? Toordokter? Is he mad? Do you believe him?"

"I am baptized. I am a Christian."

"Do you believe him?"

"He wanted me to be a *nanga*. To combine black medicine with white medicine. But I do not want to be a doctor."

"Do you believe him?"

"People—many people believe him. One evangelist visits him regularly. A Reformed pastor paid him in cash and a suit for his help. A Zion bishop depends on him for his dignity—*tshirunzi*, as we say."

"Do you believe in his divining bones? Do they tell the truth?"

"Every morning he consults his *thangu*—you call them bones. Not all are made of bones. He believes them. People believe them. I believe in God; I consult him and the Bible and my pastor. I pray to God for guidance. But my father still gives me good advice on life in general."

"So you do not believe in your father's toordoktery. You are a good boy, you do not believe in his witchcraft."

"My father is not a wizard. He practices no witchcraft. He is a good man and a good father. He works hard. But he does not go to church. My mother and I do. We pray for him. He does not always like it. He does not trust white people. Not the missionaries. He says they ridicule his religion—Mwali the Supreme Being, and the ancestral spirits. He is not a heathen, he says, nor are his people. It is not necessary to divorce Mwali to marry Jehovah. They are one. If not so, he says, why does God use him?"

"Boy, boy, boy! Do you agree with him?"

"Not on everything. Occasionally we differ very strongly on my new faith. He says the Christian faith is good, but Christians are arrogant. 'They reject everything black: religion, customs, music and musical instruments, *mirumba* and *ngoma* drums, our *zwihwana* and *mbila* guitars, our *zwitiringo* and *ndwevha* flutes, our *zwipotolio* and *miludzi* whistles, traditional dance and dress, medicine and rituals and rites and manners and foods. Everything is evil. Everything is Satan. Everything black is idol and witchcraft! Where do whites get their medicines from? From heaven or from the same trees and roots the Africans use? What is Christian about a tree or animal fat or blood or human organs? Liars. Crooks. We may prepare them differently, but what does that matter? They have taken our land. Our orchards. Our gardens. Our cattle. Now they are taking away our knowledge and skills. They will not rob me of mine,' he says."

"Your father is mad—very much beside himself. You will do well not to listen to his madness. Now 'Meneer' or 'Sir' is your white teacher at school, not me. My wife is no 'Mevrou' or 'Madam' to you. I am your Baas, and the Missis is your Missis. Do you hear, my boy?"

Tshiuda was not expected to respond, and he did not. Baas walked away: "Dunderhead, he is a very interesting kaffir."

* * * * *

He labored for three rand a month, ten cents a day. He swept, scrubbed, and polished the thirteen-room house. He washed underwear for the whole family and often tried them on himself, including the panties. He washed pots, dishes, and silverware. He worked in the garden. He washed the V.I.P. Valiant car. He helped extend the Full Gospel Church, where his baas was spiritual boss. Seven days a week, from five o'clock in the morning to late at night. There was no such thing as working hours or working conditions. Simply at his baas's beck and call. Late Saturday and Sunday afternoon brought irregular breaks, but he had to be back to wash dishes after supper. The terms "overtime pay" and "bonus" did not even exist in black labor dictionaries.

Even new machines come with instruction manuals. Tshiuda was not expected to question the content or wisdom of instructions, even those given by the nonnie and the basie. If he had doubts, he had to go to the baas or missis and say, "The nonnie—or the basie—says this, should I do it now?" If it were a stupid idea, the parents would say, "Not now. Wait till we tell you." It would never see light again. That is work. Ten cents a day. Three rand a month. Thirty days a month. Thirty-one days at times. There are not many Februaries!

Tshiuda's baas was a praying man of the Bible. A heaven-minded shepherd, he had the trust of his flock, who looked well nourished on his celestial dishes. He used the Bible to discipline his children. He used the Bible in settling arguments or starting them with his wife. She was a stout, strong-willed woman, not always obedient. He would often summon her to the pastor's study, called Mount Sinai, or he would bring the holy book to the kitchen, saying, "If the mountain will not come to Mohammed, Mohammed must go to the mountain." Tshiuda would hear him quoting the Lord in the bedroom, in the bathroom, in the garden: " 'Wives submit to your husbands as to the Lord. For a husband has authority over his wife just as Christ has authority over the Church.' It is the Lord saying it. Not I."

He had regular dialogue with the heavens. He often invited Tshiuda to listen—from outside his study room—to his most private prayer sessions, which were mostly conducted in tongues, the vocabulary a mixture of Zulu, Venda, Sotho, with an Afrikaans accent. At the end of these heated confrontations with the inhabitants of the celestial spheres, he would open the door, sporting a vaseline-like glow on his forehead, and say, "Did you understand the tongues? Does this happen in the Lutheran Church? Have you made up your mind to join the black Volle Evangelie Kerk?"

"I will think about it," Tshiuda would respond.

"What if Christ comes back tonight?" Baas would threaten. The answer was obvious: All those who were not members of the "full" gospel club, pastors and congregants, would go the way of the heathen, to the flaming bottomless hell where temperatures never fall below the boiling point.

Next door, Ezekiel (his English baas called him Francis) was the garden boy. Working with him was Saratjie, a middle-aged "kitchenmaid" and "wash-girl." They each had a room attached to the garage. When Francis would not respond to Saratjie's inviting eyelashes, Wilson, an elderly cattleboy, did. Francis invited six or seven other boys around, all of them teenagers. They would wait for the amorous couple to get into bed, then take positions at the door and small wooden windows around the room. It was not difficult to follow the intimate whispers through the thin wooden walls. Next thing, they would burst into laughter, bang the door, and disappear into the thickness of night. This was necessary, Francis argued, because the activities next to his room had caused him sleepless nights and dreams beyond his age. His friends agreed, and they helped avenge his suffering. Tshiuda also thought this an appropriate medicine. But after a month or two, only Francis and Tshiuda spent their nights alone; the rest spent their nights as Wilson did. For the first time, Wilson and Saratjie had peace.

This was an age when black boys thought black was ugly and white was all that is beautiful. They bought skin-lightening creams: Karroo. Alco. Super Rose. Atra. Ambi Special for men. Seven Days. The results were varied: Light face and black neck; red face and black lips; black-brown-light-face, black legs; pimples all over the face. They did not always have enough funds for the black-to-white project. Francis, their brainpower and idea man, came up with a solution: "*Tshilinda—muhuyu tshi linda tshi tshi la* (whoever watches over a fig tree must also eat the fruit). Why not use the creams of the missis in the house?" For those who were already trying on underwear—and there were not a few—this idea was manna in the desert. From then on Tshiuda's missis shared her mum and shampoo creams with him.

Saturday evening following month end was their high Sabbath. Led by the prophet Mapalu and disguised as girls, with tennis balls serving as breasts, they walked up and down the town streets. A few innocent prospective lovers fell for the inviting breasts and lost their teeth at the receiving end of Mapalu's fists. Later the prophet would lead them to a Zion church service, a seven-mile walk on the road to Witvlag, the black fertile country now in white hands and renamed White Flag. Their prophet always dominated the night-long prayer vigil, or *mulindelo:* preaching, prophesying, laying hands on the sick, exposing witches, and chasing after demon-possessed women into the dark, down to the river. After an hour or so, the woman would return, in her clear mind, demons exorcized. Close at her heels, the prophet would come in, singing and dancing, and the congregation would join in: "*Zion vhona madembe ahaa! Zion vhona madembe, ahaa!* (At Zion we see wonders. Ahaa! At Zion we see wonders. Ahaa!)."

Their pilgrimages to Witvlag came to a sudden and unexpected end. One day their prophet read them a letter from the Holyhorn, Lunangalukhethwa, the bishop of the Witvlag Zion Church: He could no longer tolerate wolves in sheep's clothing. His daughter-in-law, whose husband works in faraway Cape Town, is pregnant. He is holding them responsible. He has called down the wrath of God upon their prophet. He will get swollen at the wrong places. Any of them who dares visit the farm, the baas will shoot. The prophet laughed, made a bonfire of the letter, and said that he hoped a little prophet would come out of the pregnancy. Within a week, he had found another congregation where his services were needed.

* * * * *

Francis was born with a golden spoon in his mouth, but, it was said among his friends, he would never recognize luck if it hit him bang on his oval face. It was public knowledge among the "boys" that one day the nonnie, eighteen-year-old daughter of Baas Cowley, stayed away from school because she had the "flu." When her mom and dad had gone to work, and her brothers and sisters to school, she sent Saratjie to buy milk at Ciras Cafe and not at the nearby Mount Fuji, where the milk, she complained, was never fresh. Saratjie had hardly left the premises when Nonnie Linda called Francis to bring her tea and Ouma Grootjie biscuits or cookies. He had to sit on her bed and hold her tray while she drank, while her fingers chased after his ever-retreating hand. To solve the problem, he ran out of the house. She did not tell him not to tell the baas. And he did not. On several other nights, having made sure that the white world was fast asleep, Linda would knock softly on Francis's door, whisper that the baas had sent her to him to fix her bookcase. Once in the room she sat on his wooden bed without springs, mattress made of cardboard papers. In the dim light of a candle, which emitted more smoke than light, she asked him to fix her hard. She knew, she told him, that black boys were very good. Some of her classmates did it regularly. He should not be afraid. She would not become pregnant. She would provide the leathers. Even if her father came to know, he would not be too harsh. Because she had caught him twice in Saratjie's room when Mom was in the hospital for the vocal cords operation.

For as many nights as she came, so many nights Tshiuda was forced to accommodate the trembling Francis in his room. By now the Francis-Linda story had become the town talk of Louis Trichardt. Only Linda's family—and all other whites—did not know. Black boys were all saying about Francis: "*O nonelwa nga muvhuda a ri u a tula* (he is a hunter who catches a fat hare and calls it an evil omen)."[8] Francis would not be moved: he did not want a hundred bullets pumped into his tiny body, half of them in wrong places. His father had warned him before he died: "My son, you may wrong your baas in every way except one: never let your hoe plow his wife's or daughters' fields." It is our custom, Francis would say, never to go against the word of the dead.

One fateful night Linda came to his room again, as always with her passport, the bookcase, in hand. From behind the locked door, the trembling boy whispered loudly, "Go away, Nonnie. I will never do it." Linda responded, threatening, "If you don't fix my bookcase tonight, Mom will kick you out tomorrow. She wants you to fix me—my bookcase."

"Let her kick me out tonight. I am tired of running around every night. Let your brother or father fix your bookcase. Or the white basies at your school. I want to die a natural death. If you

8. Hare meat is considered a delicacy in this community. Fat hares are a rarity.

do not go, I shall call your father. I will also tell him what you have been doing to me all these months. . . ."

"Francis, come out," shouted Baas Cowley, his voice choking with rage. "Klap die nonnie . . . slap her face . . . till I tell you to stop . . . slap this bitch . . . a disgrace on my family . . . slap her again . . . stand still, you bitch . . . again, again—harder. . . ."

Linda broke away, but not before she had bitten her father's finger. She never cried. She never pleaded for mercy. She never apologized. Before sunrise, she vowed, her mother would know what happened in her room and Saratjie's room while she lay sick in the hospital.

The following week, however, Francis was promoted to foreman at Baas Cowley's garage in Tzaneen. His reputation as a "woman in man's pants" reached the garage workforce before him. He did not care. If he had not listened to *munna-a-vhane*, his late father, he would now be lying next to him at *tshiendeulu*, the burial place of the chiefs. How would he face his father and the gods and the ancestors, and Mwali the Supreme Being? Better be a woman in man's pants in Tzaneen and a real man among the gods, of whom his father was now one.

They waited for Baas and Missis Cowley to divorce; but they stuck together. They waited in vain to see Linda kicked out of the family. They guessed and speculated on why there was no explosion, until Wilson opened up: "Missis Cowley used to collect money from the Tzaneen garage thrice a week. She traveled in a bakkie truck, and came back with the bossboy seated at the back. The bossboy was fired by Baas Cowley when it was discovered he had become too close to the Missis."

On the way to the annual convention of the church at Irene, on the outskirts of Pretoria, Tshiuda sat in the back of the dark blue V.I.P. Valiant, "quality product by Chrysler," with the nonnie and the basie. At Nylstroom they had their lunch. Tshiuda tackled his quarterloaf brown bread with *amasi*, sour milk. What they ate in the small restaurant he had no reason to know. After lunch they all visited a small local zoo. There were a few baboons, a lion, and a donkey, among other animals. Pointing at the male baboon, the *tshiondongolo,* the baas said, "My boy, *daar is jou broer* (there is your brother)." Tshiuda thought one good joke deserved another and responded, "*Die gorilla is ook die baas se boetie want hy is wit* (the gorilla is also the baas's elder brother because he is white)." The baas's fury at this response clarified one thing: he meant what he said. Tshiuda knew there and then that he had lost his job. It was just a matter of time.

At Irene, whites slept in church guest rooms, caravans, tents, and hotels. Meals were served at the Conference Center. Tshiuda slept on the backseat of the Valiant and ate brown bread and sour milk—in the morning, in the afternoon, and in the evening. Occasionally Stella, a babysitter from Sasolburg, a town in the conservative Orange Free State, shared her meals with him. Her missis gave her white people's food. She also slept with Nonnie Amanda in the caravan. Her mother, she told Tshiuda, had babysat the baas when he was a child. She hoped Norah, her eldest daughter, would babysit Amanda's children. Hers and Baas Malan's family felt like one family. They never used the word "kaffir" or "baboon."

"You know," she would add, "Afrikaners are very honest people. With them you know where you stand. They mean what they say and say what they mean. If they call you baboon, you know it won't take long before they cut your tail. Unlike the English: They will use polite language. Make fine promises. Occasionally they will invite you for lunch. But, my brother, never take them at their word. They do not mean it. And when it comes to pay, forget it. Too little, and often two weeks into the new moon. If you are kicked out, you leave two weeks behind. In five years—by my brother Thembi[9]—they have thirty weeks unpaid labor."

Three of her brothers worked for the English and had the same story to tell. "Two of them are now working for Afrikaners, and one is self-employed, selling *sehlare sa banna.*[10] They were no

9. Making an oath to enhance the truthfulness of the statement.

10. *sehlare sa banna:* police-evading word for marijuana, meaning "the men's tree."

longer prepared to work for good words and empty promises. They have wives and children. They need houses and money to buy cattle for their sons' bridewealth, the *lobola.*" And, as she put it, good words will not cook for the old ladies and do not provide warmth for a tired man in winter.

One day Stella asked Tshiuda if he wanted a fifty-cents-per-night job. It would bring him money to buy fat cookies and *nyamuneithi* (lemonade) every day. Some baases needed an "eye."

"An eye?" he asked.

When she explained, he knew: Every night, from his backseat bedroom, he had seen first, black women, and after a while, white men, walking into the bluegum trees. Now he knew. They wanted him to whistle if someone suspicious walked in that direction. They did not want interference when they were busy, in Stella's words, "cutting the black bluegum trees." She also knew two black men who also regularly came to "cut white bluegum trees." He turned the offer down, not on moral grounds but out of fear. He had served once as handpost in the past, but even then the price came to him. This job froze him in his mind and melted him in his knees. When he asked her whether the police did not know, she laughed and fell on her back, making sure she fell the proper way.

"Not know? Of course they do. Two once came here to arrest, but were themselves arrested by the girls. When they get time, on duty or off duty, they come here to 'cut the trees.' They get the logs free. As long as they don't cause nonsense." She herself was not an "eye"; she got paid for recruiting "eyes."

The next day, Tshiuda was playing *khadi,* rope-skipping. His nonnie and basie lost out and left. Another seventeen-year-old nonnie, who came with her parents from Johannesburg, remained to play with him. The whole idea put shivers in his marrow. And then, lifting up the tails of her skirts, she said, "Kyk" (look). He didn't have to look. He saw. Shrunk. And walked away. A few moments later in a tent that had been vacated a day or two before, he sat alone and prayed. When he lifted his eyes and looked, he saw and again heard, "Kyk." Since the offer blocked the tent entrance, he fell on his stomach, pulled the tent pegs, and crawled away to safety. He walked to check on the nonnie and basie now asleep in the caravan. When he turned to go out, lo and behold, the offer blocked the entrance again. This time the only way to get out was to walk into it. Like Francis's father, his father Ratshilumela had warned him against playing with this type of fire. But his word did not have the strength of those below, particularly at this moment, pitted against the fire before him. In late April, Pretoria is already cold.

If he walked into the offer, he could see bullets coming from all directions. If he brushed the offer aside, pushing it out of the way, it might scream and accuse him of attempted rape. He remembered Joseph's story in Egypt. . . . If he politely negotiated his way past it, he would be, like Francis, a "woman in man's pants." When he finally found himself eating brown bread and sour milk in the company of Stella, breathing in staccatos, he had only vague recollections of how his way had been cleared. Perhaps only the angels who had grabbed Lot from Sodom had an explanation. All he remembered vividly was that two or three minutes later, the nonnie's father and his baas and missis arrived at the tent, and stood where the offer had stood. He thought to himself: at times God saves people against their will. Even those who would prefer hell to heaven—and a few bullets in the wrong places.

They spent the last night at their parents' flat. On their way to the toilet, they walked over Tshiuda where he slept in the hallway, on the carpet, under one blanket, without a pillow. The elderly people shared their meal with him, except that there was not enough room for him at their table.

At month's end, back in Louis Trichardt, Tshiuda got his wages right on time; except that it was only one rand fifty cents.

"Why?" he asked.

"We gave you a good shirt from Pretoria. A brand new shirt."

"But you did not tell me you were selling it to me. I thought it was a gift. I need my money to go back to school. You can have the shirt back. It is still in its plastic cover. I have not used it. *Asseblief*, Meneer (please, sir)."

"Meneer is your bloody f—. I do not accept shirts from kaffirs. . . . You will give this to your brother in the Nylstroom zoo. He is still walking naked. . . ."

Here the Missis and the children joined in, adding fuel to the holy fire, and within seconds the baas's whip cracked all over Tshiuda's body. As he walked-ran away, the nonnie and the basie ran alongside him: "Simon, *jy is nie meer 'n goeie boytjie nie.*" Their verdict, confirming that of their parents, was that he was no longer a good little boy.

Tshiuda thanked God at the Louis Trichardt police charge office when, behind the counter, he saw Mr. Sepolo, one of the Lutheran congregational leaders at Tshikota township. They knew each other quite well. Tshiuda's mother had looked after Sepolo's children for a long time. He himself had played and eaten with Sepolo's children. Sepolo had taught them at Sunday School. Tshiuda's sister Phophi, now a widow, had supplied Sepolo with cow dung from Halukheli to polish his courtyard.

"What can I do for you *ngwanaka*, my son?"

Tshiuda related the story to him, in detail. Halfway through the story Sepolo stopped listening, but Tshiuda did not stop talking.

"Look, my son. Go away. You cannot report on whites. They never let one another down. You go now."

Tshiuda insisted. He had been wrongfully and illegally *sjamboked* (whipped); half his wages had been withheld without cause.

"If you will not listen to me, you won't listen to your own mother and father. I don't know where you got all this madness. I know your mother and your father. Go to the white police . . . over there; but we shall not go with you . . . go!"

Tshiuda went over to the white section. At the end of his story the white officer asked for the baas's telephone number and dialed it. They spoke and laughed and greeted and thanked: "Yes . . . I see. Oh . . . that bad! I know . . . they are all like this . . . mine did exactly the same last month. . . . We shall—now . . . thank you for calling . . . thank you . . . we shall fix the problem. Totsiens . . . bye-bye."

When he turned to Tshiuda, his face was red:

"Your donder . . . you broke the Missis's *skottelgoed* . . . all plates and dishes . . . you must be thankful that Missis did not get you arrested. Baas Venter is too Christian . . . get out of my office you sk———. . . ."

When Tshiuda ran out of the office, the *sjambok* was licking at his ears, kissing selectively at the romantic parts of his body. He had tried and failed, fought and lost. Both man and the law were ranged against him, and God did not seem to care.

Under a barrage of unprintable words—Baas Venter's genuine tongues—Tshiuda collected his personal items from the baas's house and left. At the gate he walked into a new boy from the labor distribution bureau, coming to continue where he had left off, or rather, to start from square one—three rand a month. The children and their parents were waiting to receive the new one. He would be a "goeie little boytjie" for a month or two, perhaps three. Then the baas would find him a Nylstroom zoo brother. Finally the *sjambok* would crack and he would run. To another baas. From baas to baas. From baboon to bobbejaan. From three rand a month to two rand fifty. As Tshiuda would. Created to chop wood. Fashioned to draw water. Made not to be. Related to four-legged species.

What's Ability Without Opportunity?

What's man,
if nobody calls you sir?

What's a farmer
without a farm?

What's homeland,
when you own no home?

What's peace
in a land torn apart?

He's not a husband
without a wife.

She's not a widow
whose husband lives.

What's a black president
whose engine is white?

What's dangerous about the mamba,
caged in a zoo?

What's a black mayor,
when city's laws are all white?

What's a doctorate,
where color is the highest grade?

What's wrong with a tail,
if it's called a walking stick?

If wrong is righted,
and right is wronged,

Whose wrong is right,
whose right is wrong?

With no opportunities on earth,
the sky is the beginning, the earth the limit.

In a land where speech is crime,
the dumb will always be right.

I saw a millionaire
eating shrimp on the curb.

A white pauper got five bucks from him
and ate among the kings.

I saw thousands moved against their will,
in the name of their own good.

If prisoners were as happy as wardens believe,
then all wardens would lose their jobs.

A boxer alone in the ring,
landing punches against the wind, does he earn a crown?

I know 25 million people in their land,
whose citizenship is in other lands.

"If the desire to kill and the opportunity never coincided,"
would anyone ever be charged with murder?

Thank God I've never had both,
except when virtue and opportunity meet.

6

From Baas to Baas

Baas Venter had spoiled Tshiuda's special pass, invalidating it. Should he go home to get another, or should he work without one? He settled on the latter option. Special passes were limited to three a year, and he did not want to exhaust his possibilities. Several houses turned him down before he was taken on Krogh Street. No background information was required, no papers demanded, no job description. He was given a handpick and a heavy axe with which to cut wood. On the premises, at the southwestern end, stood a stack of *musimbiri* wood. At the first chop, fire sparks flew. No wonder they called it ironwood. After a good heavy lunch of porridge and fat beef, Tshiuda disappeared.

He went to the sawmills and landed a job even before he asked for it. "Go, work, we shall pay you what you are worth." At the end of the week, other special passed laborers got their pay; but the unregistered laborers were told that it had been a week of testing with no pay. This was hard on them since they had had to provide their own food and accommodations. Tshiuda slept with Isaac, his home boy; many slept under bridges.

When he got tired of the *zwikoropo,* the hit-and-go little jobs, Tshiuda decided to go home and get another special pass at twenty-five cents from the chief's place, Tshikwarani. Next day he was back at White Tom's place. Tom shelved his pass, and when all job seekers were gone, he simply said, hitting his chest, "Boy, you will work for this baas. How much?" Tshiuda wanted seven rand per month. He did not expect Tom to agree, but he hoped he would settle on five rand. Tom took Tshiuda's pass, hurriedly wrote on it, and threw it in his face. "*Gaan k*——! (go shit!)."

Under the nearby *muumo* tree, Tshiuda lay on his back, mortally wounded. For the next six months he would not be allowed to seek work anywhere in the Louis Trichardt district, for that is what the word "cancelled" on his pass meant. Black Tom came over, looked at the condemned papers, and advised: "*U luvha a hu na mapone* (paying homage to the chief does not hurt your hands)." Tshiuda got the message, walked back to White Tom, and said in a mouse voice, "I am sorry, Baas. I shall work for the baas. For anything, Baas. *Asseblief*, my Baas (Please, my Baas). *Ek is baie jammer*, Baas (I am very sorry, Baas)." Baas. Baas. Baas. That turned the tide. At the end of his day, Tshiuda sat on mowed grass in the trunk of White Tom's Opel station wagon while Tom alone occupied seats meant for five. He started work that night, at two rand fifty cents a month.

There were two boys and one cookmaid and laundry girl. Duze worked in the garden and cleaned the house. Tshiuda milked the cows in the morning and gathered them in the evening. He fed the pigs every day and cleaned the sty thrice a week, including Sunday morning. He collected pig food, *mufumbu*, leftover moat for brewing African beer, from the Tshikota location. Brewing traditional beer was illegal; but people still did it. In fact, everybody knew that those who used their leftover moat for Tom's pigs never got visits from his "tsetse flies," as his municipal police were known.

When they went hunting on Friday nights, Tshiuda carried the baas's gun; on their way back, he carried a springbok or a blesbok or an impala on his back, while the baas carried his gun. On occasion, the hit animal would disappear into thick bush, and it was Tshiuda's task to trace the blood to the prey the next day. On at least two occasions he reported no success, while each night he enjoyed the meat at his sister's place. If he had taken it to the baas, all he could hope for were legs, tripe, and the head.

Tshiuda read the Bible and Afrikaans newspapers daily. He was never able to reconcile the two.

They called the Missis *Madabadaba* (Fools) because it was her tendency to say to blacks, "*Iwe u madabadaba* (you [singular] are fools)." But she liked Tshiuda. She sent him to buy two twenty-cigarette Rothmans packets daily, for forty-two cents. Now and again he would get the change—one, two, three, four, five cents. His daily wages, at two rand fifty a month, worked out to eight cents a day, Monday through Sunday, with an occasional short rest on Saturday and Sunday afternoon.

Tshiuda's good Afrikaans made him a better kaffir than his fellow kaffirs. They did not always like him, except when he defended them against possible punishment, which was easier to do in good, compelling Afrikaans. The baas also liked him, because he kept his *mond toe* (mouth shut). The baas usually dropped groceries at another woman's place, and he hid his alcohol either behind the pigsty or among the reeds. Tshiuda kept his mouth shut on these two "great secrets" of the baas, although the Missis kept on prodding him for information. Many boys and girls in town knew both secrets. When Madabadaba confronted the baas with irrefutable evidence on both, he became furious with Tshiuda and Duze. A day later he found a good excuse to hit Duze, a short but muscular young man from Hafunyufunyu. At the end of the short, one-sided affair, the baas found himself on his stomach, calling for his gun to his unsympathetic wife. His sister-in-law, who came from across the street to see Tom blast the big head off this cheeky kaffir Duze, turned against her sister's husband: "*Tom, jy is 'n hond. Vlak op jou mag deur 'n kaffer geskop. My man sou hierdie Duze in stukkies breek* (Tom, you are a dog. Flat on your back, kicked by a kaffir. My husband would tear this Duze into pieces)." Duze left his money behind, and Tom's threats to get him arrested never came to anything. One thing was certain: Duze would never get a job in this town again.

When the days dragged on without incident, Tshiuda assumed that his uncommitted crime of betrayal had been forgiven. He was wrong. The baas probably mistook the trust and liking the Missis had for Tshiuda for a reward for his "information." In the meantime, a replacement for Duze came; but he left within a month or two.

On a Saturday in December, Tshiuda was denied his afternoon off. Standing on a stepladder against a windmill, the baas told him to grab a big bolt-and-nut iron piece from the windmill. It hurt Tshiuda's fingers and he let it fall to the ground. The baas came down, coolly picked up a shifting spanner ("bobbejaan spanner" in rude Afrikaans) and struck at the equator of Tshiuda's head. When the boy regained consciousness, the earth and all trees and houses—and Tom and his wife—appeared to dance around him. "No, Tom, you will kill him," Madabadaba was protesting.

"Laat hy doodgaan, hierdie bobbejan se kaffer se piccanin. Laat hy doodgaan." He wanted Tshiuda dead—this baboon's kaffir's pickaninny.

On groggy legs, a horn-like swelling on his head, Tshiuda went to his room and collapsed. That night he packed his personal belongings and hid them under the Bandamakwe Road bridge.

In the morning Tshiuda told the Missis that he had decided to leave, and he asked for his wages. By this time he had made a positive decision to go back to school. He had also read through the whole Bible, reviving his old desire to study theology and become a pastor. The baas came and demanded to know what *onsin* (nonsense) he was up to now and whether he had not had enough the previous day. But the Missis prevailed, and she gave Tshiuda R1.29 on this twentieth day of December. Although by this time his wages had moved up to R2.75 a month, he accepted the Missis's poor arithmetic without question. She had lived up to her Madabadaba status in doing her sums, but he did not believe that she deliberately cheated him. Perhaps it was the only change she had on her under those unpleasant circumstances.

Tshiuda moved out of the kitchen, went round the garage and toilet, and straight past the pigsty. Looking back over his shoulder, he could see Tom looking into the boys' room and then in his direction, shouting, "You must still work one month's notice!" The pigs grunted for food as he walked away—

- away from work without wages,
- away from arbitrary arrests after nine o'clock,

- away from high school students who joined the police to chase blacks for fun,
- away from *sjamboks* without end,
- away from pigs whose sties had to be cleaned on Sundays,
- away from cows whose teats they milk but never drink,
- away from Madabadaba and her ineffectual sympathies.

I Feel Like Giving In

When I look at the odds:
The mountain to climb,
The valley to cross,
The price to pay,
I feel like giving in.

When I study my opposition:
Their military gear,
The rippling muscles,
Their bloodied hands,
I feel like giving in.

When I visit the graveyard:
I see Shezi's grave;
Tshikhudo's unmarked grave,
And a space for my own,
I feel like giving in.

When I turn to my marked body
And see scars on the wrists,
Marks on the kneecaps,
And another in between,
I feel like giving in.

But for the ghost of Shakespeare:
"Cowards die many times before their death,
the valiant never taste of death but once."

7

Graduates from the University of Life

Degree I

Inspector Gezani came to Sinthumule Secondary School without warning—in the company of a white official. After the morning prayer session of the new term, the white official greeted the students and wished them a year of progress *(voorspoedige nuwejaar)* in the right direction, warning them not to follow the evil winds that are blowing people astray these days. Not to be clever to the bush.[1] He then called upon Mr. Gezani to address the students, which the latter did with an overdose of relish: "You are here for your Junior Certificates. If you allow the winds blowing from the universities—one *tshidumbumukwe*, 'Mr. Whirlwind' from the University of the North, visited here last week—to confuse you, you will end up with degrees in communism, and you know where all communists end up: jail. I am your father, I know what I am talking about."

By the time they reached their Form II class, some new students were already crying—softly. The "treatment" of "gooms," or freshmen, had begun in spite of the principal's no-nonsense warning that whoever would be caught ill-treating new students would face the full wrath of his pugilistic expertise, which, judging by his physique and finger knuckles, he certainly had. Some who did not believe him discovered the truth the painful way. The class

1. A literal translation meaning in the vernacular: do not be clever in doing stupid things.

teacher's first greeting was a reiteration of the inspector's words at prayer. She added: "If you do not hear it when told, you will hear it when you are asleep; you better listen now or never."

Class break was to prove a nightmare for the gooms. Weak-willed goom-girls "crowned" bull-willed senior boys whom they did not love. Even some well-known sufferers from womanphobia tried their luck at this fishing season, casting their nets around the insecure gym-dressed little trouts—from a safe distance on the shore, of course. Maligana thrust his letter into one trout's fin and ran for dear life. When the reply did not come for two days, he missed school for the next two weeks. Gladys found a letter in her English grammar book. She liked what was said, but she never knew the author. Student handwriting experts could avail nothing, for the enchanted lover had successfully disguised his hand.

When one endangered trout said yes to Joseph's "do you?" he did not know how to proceed; the genesis and the end of the affair merged on the spot. Madagala was whipped by a girl from Stilfontein who told him that, as an urban girl, she had no time for rural rusting *jagarumbas* or *moegies* from the *bundus*—bush-boys who did not know the difference between an English and a French kiss. She had once met a young man from a rich rural family. She had encouraged him to speak up. When she said yes, he sucked at his thumb like a baby and walked away, looking for his mother. She had had enough, the Stilfontein girl said; Madagala must get himself a bushgirl. That same day, one creative student musician came up with the Madagala love song, in the Sotho language:

When I came to Stilfontein,
I met a wondering cherry.[2]
I proposed love to her,
She narrowly missed me with a tomahawk axe,
Tomahawk, the axe of *tsotsis*,[3]
Tomahawk, the axe of *tsotsis*.

2. cherry: girl.
3. *tsotsis:* thugs.

Tshiuda found himself among two or three angry senior students who had failed their Form II.

"Mr. Distinction, let us see your report, your grades. If you know everything, do not raise your hand each time the teacher asks a question. We are not bookworms like you. You get us into trouble. We know your father had given you the 'root' and the 'bark,' these *mudzi* and *tshikwati* that make you know everything. . . ."

A rough hand grabbed Tshiuda from behind, and all his persecutors pulled back, apologetically.

"This is my meat! The king's *nama,* meat for the king."

As the feared Denga dragged him away, Tshiuda looked back, as if calling for their intervention, and could read in the eyes of Mulutanyi, one of his persecutors, "When he is finished with you, you will be a corpse." When they reached the cafe, he was told to buy bread. He bought a half loaf. They ate together. The lion and the lamb. The next day, Denga took him to the same cafe and bought a whole loaf of bread. They ate together. The lamb and the lion. Tshiuda wondered. Students wondered. The world was wondering. Only Denga was not wondering.

"Tshenuwani, I love you. From the day I heard about you, I loved you. I said to myself: I want to see *kutukana hoku* (this little boy). You are my younger brother. I have told them all not to touch you. In fact, you are not a goom. You have Form I from Mphephu Secondary School. I intervened yesterday to protect you. If anything happens, tell me. We are different, very different. Different in everything except that we are both human. I L-O-V-E you."

That day Tshiuda remembered how he had felt a strange warmth in Denga's grab the day before. In class he kept his hand up most of the time, but the little lions knew he was Denga's meat. Meat which he himself would never eat, nor allow anybody else access to. He was safe in the hands of the lion of Gededzha, probably through the intervention of the Lion of Judah.

Students sold oranges, mangoes, fat cookies, sweet corn, and anything they could sell to make ends meet. Very few had enough means to carry them through school. Had it not been for his 1965 wages, his sister's and parents' help, and these fruit sales, Tshiuda would have had to stay out of school himself.

They loved Ntonga, their teacher. Not that they hated the other teachers. But Ntonga was a special old man: hair almost always unkempt, but always well dressed. He loved very early morning lessons, and he still did well throughout the day. He reminded Tshiuda of his Standard Four teacher: "*Môre voor dinyonyana tswitswiri-tswitswiri moet julle hier wees*[4] (tomorrow before the birds sing-sing, you must be here)."

A few days before Good Friday, Ntonga went to a nearby white farmer to buy sheep, which he got at twenty rand each. But on the Thursday before Good Friday Ntonga told the class: "These Boers are mad. Last week I went to his farm on someone's donkey cart, and the price was twenty. Today we come there in a brand-new van, and the price is forty. 'After all,' the so-called Missis says, 'you kaffirs have lots of money these days. You buy vans that white people cannot afford.' While there, some whites bought the sheep—at twenty. And got a discount. I took back my money and told her to go to hell. If I were a young boy, I would end up in jail. These Boers infuriate me. Do not quote me. I have a wife and children to feed. And now, Thomas, can you recite your favorite poem, 'The Pond'?"

As if nothing had happened, Thomas stood up and said: "'The Pond': There was a little pond. . . ."

That hot January afternoon Tshiuda was on his bicycle shouting: "Lemon—mango—lemon—mango—five cent three—one cent one—fresh fresh fresh—lemon—mango—lemon—mango." At Muduluni, as he passed old Principal Kuaho's home, people rushed to him and invited him in. The radio was announcing and singing congratulations for his distinction pass. He cycled on, singing "lemon—orange—lemon—orange." But down below, he sang another song. In white South Africa they sang theirs:

4. A mixture of Afrikaans, Venda, and Sotho.

Can't Be So Bad

They sing a song of joy as they go to work,
They ululate as they weed the farms acre by acre,
How can such be unhappy?
How on earth oppressed?
Denied birthright?
In the land of their birth?
Who's so bad?
Not we,
Whites.

Staffriders jump on and off the moving train,
To the cheers of many they fall and die in song,
How can such be unsatisfied with life?
How's their freedom of movement denied?
Forbidden to dangle on death branch?
In their land of Soweto?
Who's so autocratic?
Not we,
Christians.

Down the shaft they sing *unzima lomthwalo*,
Five miles underground they sing the burden is easy,
How can such be underpaid?
They touch gold every day and every night,
Blinding diamonds shine into their dark brown eyes,
As they smash rock and granite apart,
As far as they can go.
We whites in their way?
Not we,
Civilized.

God is a government in his own right,
Who voted him into office?
All governments are from above,
  How can ours be so bad?
    Never have so few done so much for so many:
      Barbarians turned to people,
        Voters in their homelands.
          Aren't we benefactors
            Doing right?

Basotho flock across borders in full delight,
Amaswati thank their gods for a place in our sun,
  How can ours be devil's own land?
    Why feed at Satan's table?
      Even though the spoon be long?
        Where would they be without us?
          Al dra 'n aap 'n goue ring,
            Hy bly maar nog in lelike ding.[5]

Degree II

That morning Mamatho and Tshiuda went to Louis Trichardt. Mamatho picked up his suit from Permac Cleaners and put it on at Tshiuda's sister's workplace. They stopped to window-shop. An elderly white watchmaker came out of his workshop and emptied the oily contents of his dish onto Mamatho, cursing, "You want me to repair your arse, or you are just loafing kaffirs in stolen suits! Away, bloody kaffirs." Mamatho's punch caught Tshiuda on the shoulder as he jumped between Mamatho and the white octogenarian. He pulled Mamatho away, whose suit dripped oil and whose nose and upper lip twitched uncontrollably. Their old friendship, rather than Tshiuda's physical strength, actually pulled Mamatho away. If he had wished, he would have had his way and hit the man.

5. "Though an ape wears a golden ring, he remains an ugly thing."

At the police station, a black police officer handed them over to a white sergeant. Mamatho could not speak. Tshiuda could hear the singing of the boiling waters of anger inside him. He related the whole story. And then the sergeant said:

"What are your names?"

"Your addresses?"

"Your chief?"

"Your fathers' names?"

"Addresses?"

"Their baases and places of work?"

"Previous convictions?"

"Level of education?"

"Are your passes in order?"

"Places visited in South Africa?"

"Have you ever been outside the republic?"

"What books do you read?"

"Do you read English newspapers and listen to the radio?"

"What do your teachers teach you?"

"Can you always be found at home if the police want you?"

There they were: no questions about the white octogenarian. And again:

"Go home. This is just a little incident."

"But . . . what . . . little what . . . my suit . . . my dignity . . . !" Mamatho could hardly speak coherently.

"After all, you are not dead. You want us to arrest the old baas? Go, we shall speak to him."

"And what . . . how shall we. . . ?"

"Go, boys, you are now wasting my time—that is a crime—go, boys, you will hear from us. Unless you want me to arrest you for trespass . . . your school passes are not even up to date."

He hit the counter with a clenched first and picked up the phone, shouting into the receiver: "Go-o-o!"

They went. As they passed the courthouse, where the guilty are punished and the wronged vindicated, Mamatho said, coolly and unaccusing: "I knew. I did not tell you, but I knew. You should have let me fix him, that old white monkey. That is the only way to get my case to court."

"But the magistrate would never decide in your favor, would he?" Tshiuda asked in a matter-of-fact fashion.

"I don't care about these white courts with their white laws and white judges and white prosecutors. Next time you will be in trouble if you stop me from using my two trusted police officers—these fists. They are the only unbiased judges in this country. From now on I shall use them," he said, determined.

Perhaps he was right, Tshiuda thought. After all, Mamatho's Junior Certificate first-class pass meant nothing to these Boers. Not even the fact that he knelt to the same God in the black Dutch Reformed Church every Sunday.

Man-Made-Man Degree

Denga had come to Vendaland Training Institute a year before Tshiuda. Here matriculants and teachers were trained. On Tshiuda's arrival, Denga took him around, introducing him to all known goom-beaters, from room to room, and even at the local pineapple beer *shebeens*. By the close of day everybody knew that he was Denga's meat, and he went to bed as secure as the Bank of England. When tough Jacob disturbed his sleep, Cliff warned him of the consequences when the Lion would come back from quenching his thirst at Tshivhase's place. Jacob melted and flowed away like butter in an oven, to become, the next day, one of Tshiuda's closest friends—though grudgingly.

Students liked to sit on the short walls along the passageways during class break, while teachers drank their tea in separate black and white staff rooms. The white Ligwena, the big Crocodile, filled the passage with his body, his large bowlike arms dangling at his sides, students falling to his right and to his left at his unprovoked pushes. In class, at the beginning of each year, he would aim at a few selected targets, mostly students with big physiques like his, and especially those from urban areas, the "spoilt Bantu." He would empty his smoking pipe on their heads and use his fists instead of the hated lash or cane, very often without reason. One day he hit the Lion on the head with a

T-square plank. The next moment the Lion had the other end of the weapon in his hand.

"When I was wrong," he roared, "I let you beat me. When I was not sure, I let you beat me. When I have done nothing wrong, I will not let you beat me. And this time I am not wrong."

"Who is wrong, Denga?"

"You, Jombere, are wrong," Denga roared again, eyes aflame with rage.

Students jumped over desks, through the door, and out of the windows. Form Four class students looked through the cracks in the wooden divide between the Form Four and PH2 Teachers classes, and lo and behold: L versus D, teacher against student, and as the student chanting indicated, black versus white, Lion against Crocodile.

"Do you want to beat me, Denga?" asked the Crocodile, panting.

"It is you who want to beat me."

"Do you want to stab me, Denga?"

"I will not use a knife; I won't need it."

"Okay. You may beat me if you want."

"You are the one who wants to beat me."

"I did not say so."

"You did it."

"When?"

"Just now. I want you to repeat it. I will not let any man beat me for nothing. Do you eat these ones?" he said, hitting his chest with his wiry fists.

The Crocodile froze before the Lion, and when the principal arrived on the scene, he took Crocodile by the hand and walked him away. For the whole week, the Lion came to class dressed all in red, except for his dark brown shoes. The teacher's side pocket had a strange bulge, and but for the accidental blast that lodged a bullet in his thigh, students would have remained guessing about the strange object inside the disfigured pocket.

During school holidays many students worked—helping their parents or working for whites—to earn money for school fees, boarding fees, book fees, school uniforms, and pocket money. Tshiuda worked at a missionary's home, in the garden and in the orchard. Another young student worked with him, as well as a middle-aged kitchen "girl." They slept in a small room, way beyond the water and light engine, on built-in beds made of thin iron bars. On windy days the diesel smell filled their small windowless cubicle. They fed the dogs on mincemeat, while they ate *pronutro* gravy and porridge. They got seven spoons of sugar each per week for tea, but no bread.

Occasionally they stole the dog's mincemeat, and still went to holy communion. They calmed their guilty consciences by saying to each other, "If the missionary did not confess his sin of greed, we shall not confess our transgression against the Eighth Commandment. After all, we only stole dogs' meat. Dogs have no right to eat meat while we eat tasteless gravy." They not only stole the meat, they also stole the dogs' milk. So the dogs got leaner and leaner as they grew healthier and healthier, and they felt they deserved it. The dogs only barked and slept; they worked.

The children treated them very well, not always with the parents' approval. Lega bought them tinned meat and bread and gave them pocket money. She would use sign language, and they would go and pick up the stuff from her car trunk. The girls liked to sit and chat with them when they were not working, or in the evening; but always Madam would come and close the sessions with a familiar story: "It is late. You boys go and say your prayers. And you girls, come and pack your things." Next day, the girls would tell them that there was nothing to pack. In fact, they went on chatting for another two and a half hours after the jolly meeting had been dispersed at half past seven.

The missionary's only son openly and defiantly gave them all the "white" food he could lay his hands on; and he sat them on the front seat of the car, always reserved by his parents for white people. His mother's protests he brushed aside with a smile: "Mom, you are . . . ," he said, moving his hand in a circle to the right side of his head. Surprisingly, the mother never got angry with her son. Responding mildly, she would come back: "You are the one who is mad. Carrying these boys in your father's car on the front seat! No wonder they are so spoilt these days." She patted him hard on his broad shoulders.

He resembled his father, except that he was the taller and heavier giant, with a nose tilting more towards Africa than Germany, in contrast to his father's sharp nose that always seemed like it was pointing the way he walked, with a little bend, faithfully in his own fathers' footsteps, making sure he left unmistakable footprints for posterity. The father was never unduly ruffled by the son's attitude, for he knew that "when he is through with the university liberal madness, when he comes to grips with the racial realities of South Africa, then like his father and grandfather—and like all mature whites—he will know the Bantus for what they really are: their uncultivated manners, their low I.Q.'s, their barbaric culture, their incorrigible heathen practices which his grandfather and now his father have battled with the spiritual sword for decades without much visible progress."

The father's own experience as principal had taught him a few "facts" of life: blacks have no mental capacity to learn much of white people's things. There is no room for both civilization and sophistication in their brains, in their whole makeup. When black students asked him to introduce mathematics and science subjects at his school, he said, he turned that down without hesitation. He did not want black parents to drown their meager resources in planting seed on granite rock. It has no chance of germinating. As an expert on the Bantu, especially on the Venda, Tsonga, and Sotho, in that order, he knew they were incorrigible liars and incapable of logical thinking. Their best is no match for the worst in white society. It will take years, hundreds of years, before they could come anywhere near where whites were one thousand years ago.

"Look at this boy nicknamed Linger-Along. He comes to me to ask for free mangoes. He already knows I sell them. What did I do? I stood up, raised my arms, and said: 'Search me. Search me. I have none.' He left, satisfied that I had none—in my pockets. Did not even have the brain to argue back: 'But I see them on the trees.'

With such brains, can you imagine these people in a jumbo cockpit, or in a laboratory, or driving a train? I do not even trust them behind the steering wheel. Look at the increase in car accidents now that a few of their educated drunkards have cars! Without us, they all admit, even their congregations would collapse overnight. The white man is the black man's medicine. Painful truth: as Moses was God to Aaron, we are God to these people. They call us father and mother. I do not like Baas and Missis very much. But we are truly father and mother to them."

Without us:
What would they eat?
What would they have for dress?
What would they do against disease?
Who would stop their tribal wars?
And cannibalism?
You name it!

Fruit sales were doing well, first among blacks, and later white and Indian traders came to buy. Tshiuda was instructed in the morning to sell grade 3 to blacks, grade 2 to Indians and Coloreds, and grade 1 to whites. By afternoon all the grade 1 fruit was gone, all to blacks who sold again at the fruit markets along the national road from Louis Trichardt to the Kruger National Game Park. When accused of disobeying the instructions, Tshiuda said, "It is the same price for all three grades. When blacks come first, they get what is best. After all, they need more nutrition than whites. My conscience does not allow me to discriminate. Whoever comes first will get the best and the other way round." With a "you-like-arguments" frown, the missionary let him go. And when Tshiuda's time to go home and back to school came, the missionary gave him thirty-eight rand for one and a half months, quite good for a "boy" of his age.

The day he left, black pastors and evangelists and sisters were drinking tea from old jelly tins, seated on long benches on the office passage, before the annual convention started. In the days of his father, mission farm tax defaulters had their huts burned down and couples guilty of "adultery" and "fornication" were forced to cut grass along the main footpaths, and minor crimes were settled by paying fines in cattle, goats, sheep, and fowls to the missionary. This missionary had not found the need to continue the practices of his forefathers.

At high school, strikes were rare, insults by white teachers frequent. Forgetful Du Pont would often say, "I am giving you only one mark to please your mother." Oorwinnaar frowned at students from Monday through Friday, but he rarely opened his mouth in class. He knew enough about black germs and bacteria to be too generous with his gums. Students speculated that he probably got more tolerance fees[6] than all whites on the staff. Du Pont divided the class into two: dark city for dunderheads and light city for clever students. He detained them a few minutes into the break to allow lower-grade students to view who belonged where.

The students struck. That night Tshiuda and his friend were invited to Du Pont's house and fed on pawpaws and mandarin. Du Pont advised Tshiuda's friend to study journalism and Tshiuda to become a lawyer. They ate, went back, and decided to continue with the strike—until their grievances were addressed. They were addressed, but not until innocent Dennis was interrogated by the security police at Fort Edward and given lots of pork to eat thereafter. He ate. Came back. And did not change. He earned himself the name Tier (tiger).

There was another strike against bad meat and tasteless watery milk supplied by local white farmers. Students stayed in their dormitories and refused to eat. Later they came together to discuss strategies for future action. The principal, a very cool-headed man—accused by some white staff members of being infected by the liberalism of his English wife—came to the student gathering with his pocket bulging and said: "I shall

6. tolerance fee: money above salary that is paid to whites who work among blacks.

count. At ten, all of you must disperse to your classes to study. One . . . Two . . ." No one heard him say "three," for only a fool would not know the power behind the bulging pocket. Looking back at it later, Tshiuda did not think he would have shot. He and his wife were too good to be that bad. But who could tell then? In fact, most of them ran away more out of respect than fear. Probably only his thick fist was in his pocket.

The next day all the ringleaders were summoned to the principal's office at two o'clock. They stood there and waited, and by four o'clock nothing had yet happened. At five o'clock, he emerged from his office with a broad smile and asked, "What do you want at my office? Go away!" They ran from him as they had the day before—innocent and unpunished. At supper, one of his Afrikaans-speaking staff came with the boardingmaster to address the students; he concluded: "When you came here you were thin and lean and sick, as ugly as the soil of the Orange Free State. Now you are thick and fat, sparkling like a new sixpence. You even know how to use fork and knife, bastards. You do it again and I will shoot all of you." The black boardingmaster nodded assent, while the students booed and scratched the floor with their shoes. He moved on and unleashed an uncompromising humdinger blow on unsuspecting tiny, thin Differ, on whom the so-called white man's food had made no difference. That night a stone whizzed past the unfortunate boardingmaster's assistant's head, himself quite innocent. He was mistaken for the stooge, the boardingmaster.

Stooge

If he smiles,
Another is smiling.

If he walks,
His master is walking.

If he is silent,
His god is dumb.

His master is full.
His hungry stomach is satisfied.

His baas is rich.
His starving people have plenty.

"Are you happy?"
"Master, am I happy?"
"Yes, you are."
"Yes, I am."

"Apartheid is good."
"Yes, master, apartheid is the solution."
"Apartheid is outdated and dead."
"Yes, master, we've been against apartheid all along."

"I am for Gerrie Coetzee."
"I am against Tate, master."
"We've lost. Gerrie is beaten."
"We've won. Tate has won. We've lost. Gerrie is beaten."

If he passes a law,
It's Pretoria's shade.

If Pretoria's against you,
He wars against you.

When his master dies,
He ceases to breathe.

II

TSHIUDA-TSHENUWANI AND THE GOD OF SOUTH AFRICA: THE CREATOR'S CALL

8

Tshiuda in Dialogue with the Creator

Tshiuda: Did you hear Old Van Riebeeck, my Lord?
Creator: Yes.
Tshiuda: Am I in your image, my Lord?
Creator: Yes.
Tshiuda: What does that mean?
Creator: In my image . . . in my likeness.
Tshiuda: What does that mean in reality, in life situations, here in South Africa? I have spent forty years as a subhuman. I have unrestricted time to listen to your elaborate teaching if at least that will help me understand my worth in your eyes. Am I Satan's product? Tell me. Am I a distortion of your art? Tell me. Am I an accident? Tell me!

I was twelve years old when I first went to school. Teacher Munzhani asked for my name. I am Tshenuwani Tshiuda Farisani. He demanded my white name. I had none. My Christian name. I had none. He shouted at me. He wanted a name there and then. You see, I liked my two names. My first and middle names. Before me, Mother had six children, all girls. When I came, a boy, they were all surprised. "*Tshenuwani*—Be Surprised—is his name," Grandma declared. After me came two more girls. As little boys, we made toy cars of wire. Mr. Tshiuda, a black businessman, had a truck. Driving my toy car, I would sing: "Tshiuda! Tshiuda! Tshiuda!" The name stuck to me. Why did I need a white name now?

What is in a white name? I was not a Christian, Lord, why did

I need a Christian name? Is there a list of Christian names? Who keeps it? What do Jack and Piet and Dorcus mean? When Munzhani pressed, I mumbled from the back of the class, "Samson," for that was the only white name that came to my mind at that time. Next day, as he called from the register, "Simon T. Farisani," I was stupefied for a moment. "Why don't you shout 'present,' are you not here?" I succumbed, "Present." From that day I am Simon T., or some call me T. Simon. Why, Lord?

Creator: He was wrong. Your teacher was.

Tshiuda: Why, Lord?

Creator: Genesis, chapters one to three, the very beginning of the Bible, already solves this problem: *Made in my image and likeness*. I the Creator intended you and still want you to be like me. To be like me is your inalienable right. Nonnegotiable right. No individual, group, tribe, race, society, or government may interfere with this status in policy, program, or practice. Subhumans do not reflect my image; lesser beings are not in my likeness. Full persons, young and old, poor and rich, male and female, able-bodied and handicapped, literate and illiterate, of all colors, reflect my image—in sorrow or in joy, in health or ill health, in Asia and Africa, in Australia and America, in Europe and Greenland. They are shareholders in my image, heirs to my likeness. This is a gift that only I can give, a gift that no one can take away from you.

Tshiuda: Hm. Hmm. Hmmm. And now . . . ?

Creator: *Now, with it comes the right to creativity.* No person is a traffic light: red, green, amber, red, green, amber! In my scheme of things, there are no human robots. People have freedom of initiative, right of innovation, right of thought and of speech, right to do or undo. For this I gave them mind, intellect, brain, genius. They can freely choose to cooperate with my time or refuse to do so—

for birth or death,
for planting or pulling out,
for killing or healing,
for tearing down or building up,

for sorrow or joy,
for mourning or dancing,
for making love or not making love,
for kissing or not kissing,
for finding or losing,
for saving or throwing away,
for ripping or mending,
for silence or talking,
for loving or hating,
for war or peace.

Procreation is another facet of their right to participate in creation, as long as "one family does not fill the whole world alone."

Tshiuda: Yes. Yes. Yes. Now, how come that . . . ?

Creator: *Now the right to government.* Participation in government or in choosing a government in one's own country is the right that I give to all men and women. I am a democrat. I have no need to be. No one forces me to be. Nobody can. I need no human assistance to run my creation. But from the very beginning, I co-opted Adam and Eve into my cabinet to rule the world with me. People should not and cannot escape this responsibility or deny it to others. It is my command. Everybody made in my image must participate in my democratic structures. To deny people participation in government at the elective or administrative level or both is to frustrate my best intentions for humanity. There are no nonvoters in my universal kingdom.

You may call yourselves Jews, Gentiles, Moslems, Christians, Buddhists, Hindus, and Atheists, but it does not in any way absolve you from participation in the running of the affairs of this world. All will be accountable to me: Humanists. Socialists. Capitalists. Communists. Communalists. Conservatives. Moderates. Radicals. Progressives. Leftists. Rightists. Nationalists. Democrats. Republicans. Royalists. Traditionalists. All will have to account for their policies, programs, and practices. First to me, but also to their fellow citizens and fellow human beings here on earth. To shun this call is a disservice to me and humankind.

Politics is not a dirty game reserved for Satan worshipers; it is among the holiest of responsibilities. I, your Creator, am God and King. I am involved in politics twenty-four hours a day, three hundred sixty-five days a year, or sixty-six if it is a leap year. I made the institution of government. I hope you will not suggest I am involved in a dirty game. However, withdrawal of a vote or participation in a government in protest is another way of responsible participation.

Tshiuda: Does every government come from you, Lord?

Creator: Government as an institution comes from me. Just as the family as an institution comes from me. Here is a parable: A rich man had a Rolls Royce. He often traveled with his baboon. After a while, the baboon had learned a few things about operating a car. One day he took his master's key and got onto the road in the car. Now baboons are terribly afraid of snakes. And this one did not know his road signs. When he approached Chueniespoort, he saw a sign indicating sharp curves for the next two miles. To him the sign meant: "Press accelerator. Huge snakes next two miles." The Rolls Royce rolled down a cliff into the deep river, killing the driver and his family of six. The Rolls Royce, of course, was a complete wreck.

Likewise, many unlicensed baboons today are driving the institution of government without the mandate of their Creator and of their fellow citizens—with catastrophic consequences. All they know about the institution of government is that it is from God. Truly, truly, I say to you, not one baboon that drives the precious institution of government comes from God. But you are not baboons. Why is it that you oppress one another? King Saul came from me and the people. When he misruled, both I and the people rejected him. King David sinned against me and wronged his people. I punished him, and when he repented, both I and his people forgave him. Baboons don't learn. Baboons don't change. They cannot be trusted with the affairs of government.

Tshiuda: Right. Right. Right. Now starvation is . . . ?

Creator: *With regard to access to the means of living.* This coin has two sides. One side reads: "Man cannot live by bread alone." The other side says: "Man cannot live by the Word alone." For this reason I planted the garden of Eden, made Canaan the land of milk and honey, and continue to provide solid and liquid food, as well as oxygen, to human beings and animals to this day. My son Jesus did not have to deviate from Gospel Avenue to feed the hungry, heal the sick, and rekindle the spirits of the discarded. In transit from the stable of Bethlehem to Calvary, he kept his feet firmly planted—one in Spiritual Avenue, the other in Reality Avenue—and walked in such a way that the two converged. Breakfast in the morning is a God-given right; so is lunch in the afternoon; also supper in the evening. Shelter is a God-given right; dress is a God-given right.

Basic needs for life are taken seriously in my scheme of things. When you pray "Give us this day our daily bread," you mean exactly that. Overweights must, of course, avoid three meals a day. I do not advise lazy people to avail themselves at table during mealtimes. This does not include the elderly, children, handicapped, unemployed, and all others whose problems are not deliberately self-inflicted. If unemployment and inactivity are self-imposed and self-inflicted, and not a result of ill health or discrimination or natural or manmade disasters, such people will be guilty of burying my talents in a grave of indolence and passivity, of celebrating seven sabbaths a week fifty-two weeks a year.

In your situation, it is unthinkable that black people should be starving in a country that boasts of being among the largest seven food-exporting countries of the world. Your poverty and suffering, I know, cannot be attributed to laziness. You wake up two, three, and four hours before whites get up; and by the time you come home at night, they are already in bed for two, three, four, and five hours.

Tshiuda: On the farms. In hotels. In restaurants. In factories. In the mines. At the harbors. In the gardens. In their kitchens. At their laundry. On the land. In the air. On the beaches. In . . .

Creator: Your poverty and suffering is directly attributable to your color and your race. In this sense, this government finds me guilty of creating you.

Tshiuda: And of "subversion" and "terrorism" and "agitation" and "communism" and "disorderly behavior" and "endangering lives" and "breaches of security of the state" and of "interference in their domestic issues" and "imposing integrationist policies". . .

Creator: Worse still, of being Satan masquerading in God's garments . . .

A Voice: No! No! That is propaganda against our God-fearing government!

Creator: Who's that speaking?

Voice: Botha!

Creator: On whose behalf?

Voice: The South African government and people!

Creator: Which god do you fear?

Voice: Of heaven!

Creator: That God is not here.

Voice: When did we call you Satan?

Creator: Whatever you have done to the little ones of color, that you have done to me. You have discriminated against me. I have no land. I have no vote.

When I have protested, you passed legislation against me.
When I have protested the legislation, you detained me.
When I was in detention, you tortured me.
When you could not change my views, you killed me.
You pushed me from the fat of the country to the homelands.
You fed me on bogus independence.
You made me a citizen of a banana republic.
And made babies my rulers.
You banned me from my country of birth,
And called me citizen undetermined.
I was eight years and you detained me.
I asked for education and you gave me poison.
I walked to school half-naked every winter morning.
I had one brother, Hector Peterson, and you shot him dead.
I had brothers and sisters, but you forced them into exile.

I was hungry, and you fed me *kupugani.*[1]
I was thirsty, and you gave me sick water.
I became sick, and you buried me half alive.
I sat in fear as you taught me with a revolver on your side.
I was forced to spend six months in your brainwashing camp.
I had become half a zombie at the end of your program.
I threw away your pass, and you shot at me.
I became number sixty-nine of the dead at Sharpeville.
I am still in Pollsmoor as I speak to you.
I was strangled and was found guilty of suicide.
I was kidnapped and was accused of disappearing myself.
I was raped by your soldiers and found guilty of immorality.
I was your product, but you called me *colored.*
I was in the country first, but now I'm third rate.
I extracted the precious stones, and you kept the profits.
I sweated, and you took the credit.
I won, and you grabbed the trophy.
I helped you against Hitler, and you turned against me.
I got a bicycle when others got cars.
I got a fallen soldier's suit when others got fat pensions.
I had no seedbed when others got farms.
I was left out when others appeared on the Stone of Heroes.
I lost my arm and leg, but cowards got honors.
I was in El Alamein when you supported Hitler.
I am now nothing, and you are lord.
I babysat you, but now you are baas.
I washed your diapers, but now I must go to hell.
I saved you from a pool, but you shoot my child.
I loved you to earn your hate.
I hosted you and lost my home.
I became a human being to you, now I am an animal.
I trusted your god, and it stole my land.
When you despised the prophets,
When you persecuted the godly,

1. *kupugani:* gravy of poor taste and doubtful nutritional value.

When you maligned the holy,
When you scandalized the sacred,
When you mocked justice,
When you punished the innocent,
When you medaled the guilty,
When you made yourselves gods,
When you led yourself to worship idols,
When you prided yourself on the hippo and cheetah,
When you zoomed in mirages of France,
And glittered your diamond rings,
Insulting the hungry ones,
You did it to me.
Today you called me a liar,
Spreading propaganda against your country.
You are a liar, Satan is a liar.
Like Father, like son.

Tshiuda: Amen. Amen. Amen.

Creator: *The right of access to justice.* I am infallible. I am almighty. I am omniscient. I am the Eternal. I am perfect. However, I never detain people without trial. There's no coercion and torture to get confessions. No trial without truthful witnesses. No conviction without irrefutable evidence. No trial under unjust laws. No partial judge on the bench. No place for *broederbonders* on the seat of righteousness.

Adam was questioned, not interrogated.

Eve was investigated, not harassed.

Even the serpent was not convicted without evidence.

When they pleaded guilty they were sentenced, but immediately provided with a way out through sacrifice and the advocate-to-come, my Son whom I anointed the Savior of the guilty.

No life imprisonments, not even for the guilty.

Tshiuda: Does the nationalist government, from Malan in 1948 to F. W. de Klerk in 1990, respect these rights, my Lord?

Creator: How many whites in South Africa believe that blacks are created in my image? In equality? That they have aspirations, dreams, and visions? That they have five senses and a sixth for the state of emergency?

Tshiuda: That black women carry their children in the womb for nine difficult months and experience birth pains in the maternity ward? That every black child in our extended and nuclear families is an individual in his or her own right and not just one among a litter of puppies whose death is scarcely noticed by the black female, who lacks sharp maternal instincts? Do they know that the words "father, mother, son, and daughter" have their respected place in our vocabulary? That our grannies and grandpas have all the instincts of the gray-haired for their grandchildren? That *muselwa, mutanuni,* and *vhamutani* have their place of honor in marriage, as do "honey," "sweetheart," and "fiancée"?

We are not an amoral race. We have norms and values. The god of the above and the god of the below has always upheld high moral standards in our communities. Mwali did it. Dimbanyika did it. Do whites know that we can recognize a baboon when we see one? That we never mistake a light-colored gorilla for a white person as some mistake us for baboons in human disguise? We have the capacity to distinguish between the queens and kings of the mountains and ourselves—and others!

Do we not laugh? Do we not cry? Do we not embrace and kiss, even if not in miniskirts and tight pants protruding at the front? Can we not love and hate? Do we not thirst and hunger? Do we not miss our spouses when separated for months on end? Do we not know the difference between inadequate and enough, between childhood and adulthood? Do we mature, or are we always in transit?

Voice: That's malicious! It's incitement to racial tension and intergroup strife. It will not be tolerated! Not as long as I am president—executive president!

Creator: Who are you?

Voice: Botha.

Creator: Go on, Tshiuda. You may proceed.

Tshiuda: All I am saying is true, my Lord.
Some answers are found in *white* books.
Some answers are found in *white* theology.
Some answers are found in *white* education.
Some answers are found in *white* jokes.
Some answers are found in *white* history.
Good answers come out when *whites* are happy.
Genuine answers come out when *whites* are angry.
Truthful answers come out when *whites* are drunk.
Some during election time,
Some in private,
Some in public.
Some through Botha,
Some through LeGrange,
Some through Treurnicht,
Some through Terreblanche,
Some through de Klerk.
Some through slips of the tongue,
Some through posters,
Some through interrogators.
Some through doctors,
Some through magistrates and judges,
Some through informers and informants,
Some through the farmers.
Some through the business fraternity,
Some through civil servants,
Some through the government,
Others through their stooges and puppets.

The best answers are, however, written in bold letters in the transit lounges of South Africa's history. Through customs areas and beyond, many more answers are like a sewage house on top of a hill.

D. F. Malan Airport
Ben Schoeman Airport
Jan Smuts Airport
Louis Botha Airport
Verwoerd Tunnel

Strydom Tunnel
Kruger National Park[2]
Durban
Pietermaritzburg
Cape Town
Johannesburg
Pretoria
Bloemfontein
Kimberley

Hintsa City? No.
Bambatatown? No.
Tshakaburg? No.
Makhadoburg? No.
Sekhukhuni City? No.
Biko Airport? No.
Sobukwe Park? No.
Luthuli Game Reserve? Banned.
Cape Mandela? Erased from memory.
Sharpeville Memorial Square? Over my dead body!
Peoples' Liberation Stadium? *Dit sal die dag wees!* (That will be the day!).

Who are we, Lord?
Who will name places after apes?
No history behind us,
No future ahead of us.
No city in our name,
No park in honor of our heroes.
No tunnel. No airport. No bay. No cape. No nothing in our name. Nothing. Nothing. Nothing!

Now, my Lord, life is a relay race. I am already tired—and am trembling at your presence. Tshenuwani has now agreed to take you through life as it is in South Africa.

He will take you to the transit lounges. To customs.

2. Kruger National Park: a game reserve.

To the check-in counters. To downtown. And beyond, where your angels fear to tread.

In Creation Transit Lounge

Voice: I object very strongly. God is for heaven, and earth is for us. You have no right to take him through my country. It's interference in our domestic affairs. Does he have a visa?
Tshenuwani: The world and all that is in it belong to the Lord; the earth and all who live on it are his. He built it on the deep waters beneath the earth, and laid its foundations in the ocean depths.
Creator: Who is that?
Voice: President and the First Lady.
Creator: Will you repeat yourself?
Voice: Your application for entry visa to my country is granted on condition:

You come after sunrise on Sunday and leave the same day before sunset.

You travel straight from heaven to the Waterkloof Nederduits Gereformeerde Church.

Only white angels are included in your entourage.

Your sermons do not deviate from the official theology on race relations.

You do not overstay our hospitality.

Creator: Who are you?
2nd Voice: Minister of Law and Order, instructed by the First Citizen. He is here with me.
Creator: I want to visit many places and many people.
Law-and-Order: At whose invitation?
Creator: I have seen how cruelly my people are being treated in Apartheidland; I have heard them cry out to be rescued from their slave drivers. I know all about their sufferings, and so I have come down to rescue them from their murderers and torturers and exploiters. I shall take them out of detention and

cancel their life imprisonment. I shall take them out of apartheid ghettos and barren homelands into a new country that I shall create for them: a united, democratic, nonracial South Africa, a fertile and spacious land, a land of milk and honey, a land of gold and diamonds, a land rich in fauna and flora, a land pregnant with limitless possibilities. In the new South Africa, black and white will live and work side by side, sharing woolen blankets in winter and ice cream in the summer sun. Mandela and de Klerk will ride on the same motorbike. Tribe will live side by side with tribe, because divide-and-rule ideologues will give way to black and white leaders in whose veins flows the blood of unity. On that day my people shall no longer sing: "Every tribe and every race for herself and God for us all." The new song shall be the old banned song: "Unity is strength/*eendrag maak mag/motho ke motho ka batho/Umntu ngumntu ngabantu/muthu ndi muthu nga vhathu.*" Artificial racist boundaries and laws shall disappear from the statute book as darkness does at sunrise. I have indeed heard the cries of my people, voices of ten thousand children in detention! I have seen how modern-day Egypt is oppressing them.

Law-and-Order: Your transit visa is withdrawn with immediate effect.

Creator: Who are you?

Law-and-Order: Minister of Law and Order. Under instructions.

Creator: Under which act do you act against me?

Law-and-Order: Section 40(1) (c) of the Admission of Persons to the Republic Regulation Act, 1972 (Act 59 of 1972); and Section 2(b) of the Aliens Act, 1937 (Act 1 of 1937).

Creator: But those are the acts under which you have restricted one of my pastors. I am not a person. Those acts cannot apply to me.

Law-and-Order: Are you not three persons in one?

Creator: I am. Your theology is quite good.

Law-and-Order: Right, and you are banned under the same act. What's good for the goose is good for the gander.

Creator: That is not what the acts say.
Law-and-Order: That's parliament's intention.
Creator: Is that all?
Law-and-Order: No. I also ban you under the Prevention of the Violation of Two Kingdoms Act, which leaves the heavens to God and the earth to men. Your privilege to visit our country is withdrawn.
Creator: Is that all?
Law-and-Order: No. I also ban you under the Bantu Influx Control Act.
Creator: But I am no Bantu. And that law is repealed.
Law-and-Order: No Bantu? That's good for you. But still, you are a kaffirgod and a kafferboetie, their real brother.
Creator: But the law is repealed!
Law-and-Order: Then I ban you under the Orderly Urbanization Act of 1986.
Creator: But I want to spend most of my time with the hungry, the sick, the strangers in their own land, the naked, the prisoners, those on trial, the police-made widows and orphans. I want to visit the graves of unrest victims, of children who die of malnutrition before age five in a country of plenty and overfed dogs. I shall be in black areas most of the time.
Law-and-Order: That's very dangerous. God among blacks? That's how the liberals spoil our good Bantus. You are banned further under the Political Interference Act. Now go or risk detention! *Hoor!*[3]
Creator: I sent my prophets, and you did with them as you pleased. You banned people. You banned books. You banned organizations. You banned newspapers. You banned ideas. You banned movements. You banned justice. You banned prayers. You banned sermons. My people tried negotiations, demonstrations, civil disobedience, industrial strikes, consumer boycotts, rent boycotts. You crushed them. You mowed them down. You did it yourself. You used vigilantes. You employed instant police,

3. *Hoor:* Do you hear!

your *kitskonstabels*. You used brutal surrogate homeland forces. You insulted the Eminent Persons Group. You closed all peaceful avenues of change. Arrogant. Stubborn. Incorrigible.

Law-and-Order: That's a misunderstanding. Just as the whole world misunderstands our good intentions. When our policies are implemented to their logical conclusion, many nations will turn around to congratulate us. To learn from us.

Creator: You play with words. You practice doublespeak. Today you call on liberation movements to renounce violence. You call on Mandela to do the same. If they do, you say you will negotiate. They call upon you to stop your violence, structural and physical. To sign a ceasefire. To release political prisoners. To let exiles come home. To withdraw your brutal forces from among my people. What is your response? Bombing raids on neighboring states. Declarations of states of emergency. Disguised martial law.

Law-and-Order: But for reform to succeed in an evolutionary fashion, we need calm and stability, law and order. We shall not succumb to the wild demands of revolutionary Marxists whose sole goal is to make our country a one-party communist dictatorship.

Creator: Presently you are a democracy . . . ?

Law-and-Order: Yes, but we are still evolving . . .

Creator: From animals to humans?

Law-and-Order: Not exactly . . . but our Bantus need time to evolve from a cannibalistic-primitive-cultural-ethnic state to the middle phase of civilization and then to move on, developing the capacity to understand the period of Renaissance and the era of Enlightenment, after which they need to learn good manners about dress and housekeeping and to respect their wives and not to spit in the street and how to use money well—not like now when they use all their money for liquor and women—and to fight witchcraft. Without us they would slaughter one another . . . if we give you a permit to visit Soweto you will walk among corpses in the street, some without ears and some without private parts . . . it is surely a long journey before we make these people human, and violence is the only language they understand . . . their skins are hard like elephant hide and their big heads are full of sand. . . . I need not tell you, for you know much about how differently you created some of these people.

There lies the problem. We are willing to defend this truth at all costs: South Africa, our fatherland, for you we shall die, for you we shall live. Even if the whole world and God do not help us, we are willing to fight the devil alone, with all the means at our disposal. We shall flush him out of his hiding places in our country, and we shall hit him wherever he plots his rape and murder of our people, even if we have to hunt and destroy him in the countries that harbor him.

Creator: Are you really alone? Your spare parts? Your military technology? The cheetah bomber? The atom bomb? Are you really alone? Your armies will not save you against me. Vetoes at the United Nations will not prop you up forever. Let my people go. Don't wait for Passover, as Pharaoh of old did, to his regret.

Tshenuwani: Like his *volk*, he bases his arguments on creation, my Lord. Let us go into real life. Into South Africa!

Law-and-Order: Then my government is willing to compromise and take you on a guided tour. Free. On condition Tshenuwani stays behind. We shall not take rabble rousers.

Creator: You want to guide me?

Law-and-Order: Yes.

Creator: I require a visa to visit South Africa?

Law-and-Order: It's the law.

Creator: A transit visa?

Law-and-Order: Whom can we trust?

Creator: You don't trust me?

Law-and-Order: Even gods can disappoint. Meddlesome.

Creator: I am one among many gods?

Law-and-Order: Let's agree to disagree. I am implementing the law of the country.

Creator: That's above my law?

Law-and-Order: Every king is king in his own country. Every cock is king on his dung heap.

Creator: That applies to me?
Law-and-Order: The god we worship is law abiding.
Creator: Obeys *your* laws?
Law-and-Order: He made the laws—the commandments—blessed Shem and Japheth and cursed Ham.
Creator: And?
Law-and-Order: At the Tower of Babel separated people into their races and tribes and colors. Whoever brings together that which God separated works against God's best intentions for humankind.
Creator: And?
Law-and-Order: Some are born rulers. Others to chop wood and draw water. God does not make mistakes. It was good in his eyes that Canaan served Israel.
Creator: And?
Law-and-Order: In Acts, chapter two (that is, if you need a reminder), the Holy Spirit recognized and respected all ethnic groups and their languages. God and his Spirit are orderly. No disorderly mixing of things that essentially do not belong together. Look at the busing thing in America: lowering of standards everywhere. Blacks cannot keep the white man's pace. It is not their nature. They are made differently. Meant for other things. In Afrikaans we have a saying: "Although an ape may wear a golden ring, he remains an ugly thing." There are so many plane accidents in America. And Africa. Why make pilots out of people engineered for donkey rides and presidents from material created for servants? I shall not take the blame for their low I.Q.; I did not create them.
Creator: I shall. Whoever insults the I.Q. of the creature insults her/his maker. Tshenuwani, read Genesis 1:26-30.
Tshenuwani: "Then God said, 'And now we will make human beings; they will be like us. They will have power over the fish, the birds, and all animals, domestic and wild, large and small.' So God created human beings, making them to be like himself. He created them male and female, blessed them, and said, 'Have many children, so that your descendants will live all over the

earth and bring it under their control. I am putting you in charge of the fish, the birds, and all the wild animals. I have provided all kinds of grain and all kinds of fruit for you to eat; but for all the wild animals and for the birds I have provided grass and leafy plants for food'—and it was done."

Creator: My Son, almost two thousand years ago, said something relevant to this. Tshenuwani, read Matthew 6:25-32.

Tshenuwani: "This is why I tell you: do not be worried about the food and drink you need in order to stay alive, or about clothes for your body. After all, isn't life worth more than food? And isn't the body worth more than clothes? Look at the birds: they do not plant seeds, gather a harvest and put it in barns; yet your Father in heaven takes care of them! Aren't you worth much more than birds? And why worry about clothes? Look how the wild flowers grow: they do not work or make clothes for themselves. But I tell you that not even King Solomon with all his wealth had clothes as beautiful as one of these flowers. It is God who clothes the wild grass—grass that is here today and gone tomorrow, burnt up in the oven. Won't he be all the more sure to clothe you? What little faith you have! So do not start worrying: Where will my food come from? or my drink? or my clothes? Your Father in heaven knows that you need all these things."

Creator: What do you learn from the Genesis text?

Tshenuwani: That God made one human race in his image. Human beings were such from creation. There is a clear distinction between human beings and animals; one does not evolve from the other. All human beings are invited to rule this world and subdue it, not to subdue one another.

Creator: And from Matthew?

Tshenuwani: God wants all human beings to have food and clothing. All human beings are precious in his eyes; they are worth much more than animals and plants. God wants us to trust his providence. Unless people become greedy, in this world there is food, clothing, and shelter for everybody.

Creator: Go and believe that! Teach that! Preach that! Live that! Challenge and refute all teaching that subverts that.

Tshenuwani: But my Lord . . . who am I . . . a boy . . . son of a . . . my mother used to do the *malombo* dance[4] . . . you heard the Voice—the powerful voice . . . and Old Van Riebeeck . . . I cannot . . .

Creator: Do not say that you are too young, but go to the people I send you to, and tell them everything I command you to say. Do not be afraid of them, for I will be with you to protect you. I, the Lord, have spoken.

[*Then the Lord reached out and touched Tshenuwani's lips.*]

Listen, I am giving you the words you must speak. Today I give you authority over nations and kingdoms, to uproot and pull down, to destroy and overthrow, to build and to plant. . . .

I will punish my people because they have sinned; they have abandoned me, have offered sacrifices to other gods, and have made idols and worshiped them. Get ready. . . .

Go and tell them everything I command you to say. Everyone in this land—the kings, the officials, the priests, and the people—will be against you. But today I am giving you strength to resist them. You will be like a fortified city, an iron pillar, and a bronze wall. They will not defeat you, for I will be with you to protect you. I, the Lord, have spoken.

Tshenuwani: You have spoken, Lord. Let it be.

4. *malombo:* ancestor-spirit-filled dance.

III

TSHENUWANI ANSWERS THE CALL

9

The Gospel Ministry

I always wanted to be a pastor—from that fateful day when I met Hanna Lechler, a German missionary, at a children's service in the small Muduluni church. I had just won her Bible story contest when she said: "The candy you have won is sweet, but God has given us a sweeter thing. In his love, he gave us his son Jesus Christ." With these words she distributed the candy also to those who had not won the contest, adding, "In Christ, there is sweet life for everyone. We do not win it; it is a gift, a gift of grace." I fell in love with this gospel, and except for the shaky period in Form Three when I was nearly derailed to learn sisal weaving, I wanted to preach it. I owe my thanks to Ratshilumela and Elelwani Khuba, my teachers who gave me invaluable advice at a critical moment in my life.

We loved our time at the Lutheran Theological College, Umpumulo, the place of peace. However, a few things disturbed our shalom: discrepancies between the salaries of black and white staff, the rock-bottom wages of the kitchen staff and gardeners, the separation of black and colored student dormitories, the tendency of some white lecturers to travel miles to a German congregation at Hermannsburg while a black congregation was hardly a mile away. During our time there were a few exceptions to these views and practices: the Lochmanns, Kamphausens, Sundermeiers, and Homdroms.

Some of the theological teachings were also highly suspect: "God created the lion to feed upon the buck. Why should blacks complain about white oppression?" "Everything is the will of God. I am rector. Very often I work until late at night. I do not complain. In whatever position you find yourself, God's will has placed you there. Do not complain." "Do not waste your precious time on so-called community development projects. There is plenty of work on college grounds during manual work hour. Lots of papers to pick up. We do not like the evil spirits of secularism planted by SASO[1] in our college. It disturbs the spirit of cooperation. We do not welcome the *spiritus mundi* here."

Through the Student's Representative Council, the SASO executive, the Food Committee, and the college magazine *Focus*, we challenged racism on holy ground. One article was entitled "The Paradox of the Holy City." On March 29, 1972, Johannes Ramashapa and I, both students, were suspended from the college. When the black vice-principal, or prorector, came to tell me to leave, as the rector had instructed, I simply said, "Go away, Judas." He became furious and threatened to let loose his sons on me if I repeated it. I repeated it thrice, "Go away, Judas." He left, fuming. But he, and only he, knew what I meant. In private he had encouraged us; now in public, to win the white man's favors, he had turned against us.

Toward a Doctorate-in-Life

The church council did not find me guilty: white Bishop Pakendorff did not side with his German brothers. He warned me to be careful, to stay clear of hot issues, to avoid conflict with the state. This reminded me of the words of chief minister "Mina" at the Missiological Institute at Umpumulo: "My boy, if birds play too close to the windmill wheel, they get cut and killed."

When I did part-time work as court interpreter during college vacations, Magistrate Marais put me in the backseat of the car,

1. SASO: South African Students' Organization.

for blacks could not sit with whites in front. On our way to Soekmekaar, Bandelierkop, Alldays, Marabuys, Waterpoort, Levubu, or Louis Trichardt, I would buy a newspaper, throw my body lazily on the seat, and read. Whereupon he moved me to the front seat; and although he said nothing, I knew he did not want to look like a black man's chauffeur. The next day, he warned me not to think too much of myself, not to read until my head was full of nonsense. I must not play too close to the fire. The white man can provide warmth in winter, but he can also burn and consume if provoked. He hoped he would not need to give me another lecture.

One day, returning from Soekmekaar, the car hit a guineafowl—which broke the windshield—and swerved into a fence and stopped. We removed pieces of glass from each other's eyes and ears, and pieces of torn guineafowl meat from each other's clothes. Bird blood had splattered all over our clothes. We shared what remained of the bird equally, unlike the way we share our country and its resources. Together, side by side, we pressed our chests against the car and pushed it back on to the road, unlike the way we refuse to work together to save our country from the racial time bomb.

As we parted that day, he said, for the first time, "Good-bye, Mister Farisani. Get yourself sick leave tomorrow, paid sick leave. We nearly died together." I said, "Good-bye, Mr. Marais," no longer "Magistrate Marais." We had been that close, skin against skin, black for white and white for black. The white man's fire did not burn or consume me, nor did the black cannibal mistake his pale skin for guineafowl meat. If guineafowl blood can bring us this close, what neutralizes Christ's blood, which we drink every Sunday but stay millions of light years apart?

I served the Madabani congregation assigned to me; then the Muraleni and Madodonga congregations were born. For a while I was a stopgap teacher at my former secondary school, Sinthumule High. Later I was seconded to the Bible Society to work on a new Venda version of the Bible. In the meantime, I also became the president of the Black People's Convention (December 1973), and the following year also of the Bold Evangelical Christian Organization. But by early 1975 our white coordinator had engineered the dismissal of Mahamba and me. Behind this dismissal lay skeletons of racial bias—and insults, threats, and manipulation. The people who voted us in were overruled; the unelected remained in the driver's seat, guiding the translation against the people's will, probably against God's will.

* * * * *

I came to Beuster as center director. But no one came forward to introduce me to the work. The minutes of discussions showed that the whites in charge and their committee did not want an independent thinker. I was not allowed to park my car under the missionary's tree garage, and I was billed for staying at the center with my cousins.

The Diocesan Council wanted Tshakhuma Home Industries run by an elected committee. The whites in charge protested and refused to enter into an official handover, or to share information about the donors or funders of the project. It was the missionary's family project, they argued. When a black committee took over, all credit facilities, formerly available to white management, were withdrawn. At whose recommendation?

German partners were scheduled to visit one of our parishes. The missionary's family wanted to fetch them from the airport and to accommodate all six. The feeling of the circuit was that partnership involved both the congregation and the black pastor. The missionary's daughter protested vehemently, with her mother's support: she wanted to go alone. The black pastor will come late on the day of departure, she said. He will not get accommodations in Pretoria. Then, finally, Okay, she will take the pastor with her, against her will, but only because the dean dictated it.

When funds arrived from overseas, canvassed in the name of black congregations, they were kept in personal accounts and dished out in bits and pieces at the missionary's whim. The congregation never participated in administering the funds—and was scarcely informed of the amount or the donors. At times they were told to submit the budget of their needs, which Father or Mother Christmas met; or they were told to go and buy and send the account to the benevolent Mother to settle. Letters of thanks were expected, but they would be channeled to the donors, unknown to the beneficiaries. It goes without saying that projects funded this way:

- crumble when Father Christmas dies;
- collapse when handed over to black management;
- never have their funds audited;
- create and encourage dependence on the "Father" or "Mother," but never promote creativity and self-reliance;
- do not promote the functioning of God's church as a body of Christ, working together, sharing joys and sorrows, information and responsibilities. Members of the same body do not keep one another in darkness, and one member does not strive to be the head of the body, or Father Christmas; that is reserved for Jesus Christ.
- never promote mutual trust;
- promote master-servant, boss-boy relationships, and is a concrete expression of apartheid in the church;
- sabotage black initiative, and play into the hands of those who use black misery to enrich themselves while continuing to rob blacks of their humanity and dignity;
- give financial muscle to those who want to buy influence and manipulate black opinion in the church;
- violate the regulations of the church, which the black clergy is expected to follow to the hilt while whites have total immunity;
- constitute a practice that is dangerous medicine, and is ineffective against Satanitis.

I Am Not a Politician

Yesterday I wanted all these white ants killed,
Today I want them all saved.
They have to die for they killed our people.
Without death we are without freedom.

They must live—because Christ died for them!

Last year I called them all devils,
Today I know some are angels.
They are devils for they behave like devils,
Without throwing them into hell we'll never see heaven.

They'll repent—because in Christ nothing is impossible!

Last week I called Botha an incorrigible racist,
Today I believe there's a silver lining in this racist cloud.
He is incorrigible for he never bends,
Without breaking him we'll never break our chains.

He'll change—for he is now headed for Damascus!

Last month I invited all of you to war,
Today I believe in the way of peace.
War! War against the warmongers.
Without war peace will never come.

God will beat swords into plowshares!

In my anger I opened floodgates of wrath,
Today I want to stem the tide.
Throw all these fascist racists into the ocean.
Unless they drown we'll never emerge.

Man's anger does not work the righteousness of God!

10

Through a Minefield of Racism

Our ancestors said: "*Nowa a i na nowana,*" and rightly so, for every little snake is still a snake. It can kill. It is not a mambalet. Or puffadderlet. Or snakelet. Our ancestors could have said, "*Apartheid a i na apartheidana,*" for there is indeed no such thing as great or small apartheid, grand or petty apartheid. Discrimination is discrimination, whether you call it separate development, parallel development, self-development, homeland policy, self-rule of black independent states, or group rights. *Apartheid a i na apartheidana.* No such thing as apartheidlet.

Race and Toilet

I entered a toilet at L.T.T. Motors in Louis Trichardt on my way from church council. Pastor Phosiwa walked to buy food at Cira's Cafe. The baas left his lunch and pushed to open my door. When I was done, I opened. With knife in hand, this hefty man threatened to cut my throat and my pastor's collar for daring seat "my ass on the white people's toilet." I looked straight into his eyes and told him to do as he pleased. When he would not proceed, I walked past him to my car. Encouraged by the looks of his wife and the look in his children's eyes, he turned to me again and emptied threat after threat. I looked into his eyes again. "This is our country! These are the black man's toilets. This is our town. Next thing we shall be in parliament making laws for you. You are wasting your time. Go, phone the police."

When I left, I saw him talking to the black petrol attendants, probably telling them that that night I would sleep in a cell. It was late 1985.

Sometime in early 1986 we advertised our need for water drillers. One day, when I opened my office door, a white man walked in and asked for Dean Farisani. In my dirty shorts and undersize sweater, having spent that morning in the garden, I did not look like a dean. Where had I seen this man? I asked him what he wanted.

"I go around drilling water. I hear the Lutheran church needs boreholes. I want to speak to the dean."

What is it that makes him so humble and so shy? So unlike whites? I told him that I was the dean, and invited him to take a chair. I ordered coffee. After looking through his rates, I asked him, and he agreed, to start the next morning. But he did not come the next morning. That afternoon I met him in Cira's Cafe. He tried to avoid me, but did not have enough time to hide behind the shelves. He blamed his van for the nonappearance. A few minutes later, I visited my L.T.T. toilet. When I came out, I asked about the "toilet boss," as I now called him.

"When they got your letter, they came and we told them what happened. They asked him to apologize and he refused. They told us to remove the Whites Only sign."

"Who?" I asked.

"People from the big head office in Johannesburg told people in the small head office in Pietersburg and they came."

"Where is he now?" I asked.

"He is drilling water. In your area. Just now we saw him walking into Cira's Cafe."

When I had written a protest letter some weeks before, threatening never to get gas from their station and to influence other people to do the same, I had never thought action would follow. In fact, the petrol attendants told me that the toilet boss had nearly been stabbed by a Jo'burg man when he tried to get him out of the toilet. He locked himself in his car. At Sibasa, one black man who knew him dragged him—pants at knee level—out of a black toilet.

At Northern Motors my wife and little children went into the ladies' toilet, and I went to the other one. When I came out, a black salesman, sent by a white saleslady, opened his mouth to say something. But I told him not to say a word, but rather to call the white lady to do it herself. She did not come.

In Pietersburg I walked into a public toilet at a garage. An elderly man asked what I wanted to do.

"I have a permit," I said, closing the door behind me. When I came out, he was waiting at the door.

"From whom?" he asked.

"From God!"

I left him open-mouthed, and when he got his vocal machine together, he shouted at my back: "Cheeky!"

At Checkers Supermarket, our children wanted to respond to the call of nature.

"No," said the black man in charge of toilets, "there are no toilets for Bantu, Indian, or colored."

I asked him to take me to the boss responsible for that policy. At a safe distance, he pointed with a head movement "there" and disappeared. When the white boss did not respond to my knock, I opened the door of his glass office.

"I understand you are in charge of the toilets. How do I get there?" I asked.

He froze in his chair and mumbled something like, "You turn right, then left, and again left. Ask the toilet boy to show you the way." When I turned, I heard a heavy sigh of relief: another troublesome kaffir!

Race and Restaurants or Cafes

We walked with old P. R. Ngwana into a restaurant. We served ourselves and went to the counter—P. R. to the black pigeon hole and I to the white counter. The ever-pregnant white woman served P. R., then took my items to the black counter and told me to pay from that side. I refused. She called her husband, who came fuming.

"Kaffir, are you coming to buy or cause trouble? I will kick your head out of your neck, you hear?"

I responded in immaculate Afrikaans:

"*Ek is ewe oortuig dat ek presies dieselfde aan u kan doen, Meneer* (I am equally convinced that I can do exactly the same to you, sir), and since we do not know the outcome, we had better not try it."

We stared into each other's eyes and, without a word, agreed to compromise. I walked away empty-handed, and he did not try to make me pay for the items that his wife had already ticked away on the cash machine. When I stopped at the same white counter a few days later, the husband came over, ticked away my items quickly, and then said:

"You are a chief. I think I saw you with Chief Mphephu one day."

I nodded to his lie and walked away, a chief without a country.

Race and Driving

At Tshakhuma, the white traffic officer checked my car thoroughly. When he found nothing wrong, he said,

"*Jong, waar het jy die kar gesteel?* (Boy, where did you steal the car?)."

"Where did you steal your traffic officer's certificate?" I asked. A battle of words, but no casualties.

I was driving at 120 kph when a white cop stopped me for speeding. "You will pay two thousand rand, get your license revoked for five years, and spend two years in prison. Go away, do not do it again." I thanked him and drove to my next church service, at the Tshikota location. When the Presbyterian congregation at Shirley, where I preached that morning, heard it, they thanked the Lord. Baas Trompies was known for overkill, not grace. Did Tatane Mabinda not pay two hundred rand for doing ten miles over the limit?

Between Potgietersrus and Pietersburg they stopped me. Without a word, the cop started writing a ticket.

"This case will go to the appeals court in Bloemfontein," I protested.

"Why?"

"That car before me—I have the license-plate number—triggered the speed trap, and you let the white man pass and are penalizing me for his crime. I shall fight this case to the bitter end."

He stopped writing.

"What work do you do?"

"Is it necessary?"

"Bring out your pass." I gave it to him.

"Oh, you are a pastor. My father was a missionary in the Lutheran Church too. We are brothers. I do not like apartheid. Sorry for the inconvenience. I shall cancel this ticket."

Church and State

When I came, the elders were seated, enjoying cakes and tea on the green grass. When I took my chair, they all left theirs. The man of God in Pretoria apologized on behalf of himself and his wife, and after we prayed, I left.

We were on our way to West Germany. From our hotel in Hillbrow we phoned a friend, Dr. Kistner, who gave us the address of the local Lutheran congregation. However, the congregation's pastor would not see us; he had confirmation class. With our child we went to the service the next morning. Everybody frowned at us, and at the end of the service, the pastor walked past, looking at the floor before him, and never greeted us.

Old Bishop Giesekke took me to a white Lutheran congregation in Louis Trichardt. He never succeeded. Nobody was willing to talk to me.

Our white missionary friends wanted me to baptize their child in the white Lutheran church in Pietersburg. They failed. Just as I failed to convince their pastor to visit our congregations. The baptism took place in the nearby Anglican church. When University of the North black Lutheran students visited the congregation in early 1986, a son of a missionary, among others, walked out in protest against the black presence. He later apologized, so we learned. To whom?

* * * * *

In June-July 1984, in Budapest, the Lutheran World Federation suspended the white Lutheran churches in Namibia and South Africa for practicing apartheid in the church of God.

STATEMENT ON SOUTHERN AFRICA:
CONFESSIONAL INTEGRITY

The Assembly adopted the following statement on the recommendation of its Business Committee and after a lengthy open hearing at which all parties concerned had the opportunity to present their points of view.

The Seventh Assembly of the Lutheran World Federation, having studied and heard extensive reports regarding the situation in Southern Africa:

1. REAFFIRMS the resolution of the Sixth Assembly (Dar es Salaam 1977) on Southern Africa: Confessional Integrity.

2. STRONGLY AND URGENTLY APPEALS to its white member churches in Southern Africa, namely the Evangelical Lutheran Church in Southern Africa (Cape Church) and the German Evangelical Lutheran Church in South West Africa (Namibia) to publicly and unequivocally reject the system of apartheid (separate development) and to end the division of the church on racial grounds.

3. Regretfully concluding that no satisfactory fulfillment of this goal has as yet been achieved, FINDS that those churches have in fact withdrawn from the confessional community that forms the basis of membership in the Lutheran World Federation.

Therefore, the Assembly is constrained to SUSPEND THE MEMBERSHIP of the above churches, intending that such action serve as a help for those churches to come to clear witness against the policy of apartheid (separate development) and to move to visible unity of the Lutheran churches in Southern Africa.

4. UNDERSTANDS that suspension means that those churches are not entitled to send voting delegates to an LWF Assembly or official meeting, nor to have any of their members on a governing organ of the Federation.

5. INSTRUCTS the Executive Committee to lift this suspension if satisfactory actions are taken by the churches involved to establish the legal and practical conditions for abolishing the practice of apartheid in the life of the churches and their congregations.

6. OFFERS the Lutheran churches in Southern Africa every support and assistance as they seek to witness to the gospel of the grace of Jesus Christ and move to visible unity. Such support and assistance should include the following:

a) A visit of a delegation of the Federation to counsel with and encourage the Lutheran churches of Southern Africa.
b) Encouraging other regular visits to the churches by other member churches and the Federation.
c) Continued appeal to member churches around the world to support all Lutheran churches and all churches in Southern Africa in prayer.
d) Continued commitment to strong advocacy on the part of the LWF and its member churches, seeking to support peaceful and positive change toward the equality of all people in the societies of Southern Africa.

7. ENCOURAGES all member churches to engage in ongoing self-examination in the light of Scripture, rejecting all forms of racial discrimination.

Working group 10: RACISM IN CHURCH AND SOCIETY

The introductory paragraphs to recommendations made by the working group were received by the Assembly and are reprinted here in order to document a summary of the discussion that took place in the working group. Boxes are used to highlight the actions taken by the Assembly on the basis of the report of the working group and subsequent discussion in plenary.

i) Racism

All people are created in God's image. In Christ, the creation broken by sin is restored to fullness as people are reconciled to God and to one another. Through God's gift of the Holy Spirit, the people of God's church are empowered to live as one people celebrating the fullness of God's creation. In Christ all divisions among people are broken down. The church is God's instrument for reconciliation in the world also as it witnesses through its life to the new creation in Christ.

Apartheid (separate development), the most violent of racism's institutional forms, is an ideology that a) denies the church's doctrine of creation; b) denies the gospel of reconciliation; and c) is a roadblock to the work of the Holy Spirit in the lives of people who have made race a criterion for human relationships. It establishes exclusive privileges for some at the expense of others. It creates a situation of injustice and violent oppression causing suffering and death to millions.

ii) Racial discrimination in Southern Africa

Apartheid, therefore, is incompatible with the gospel. It incurs the anger and sorrow of God. It is a heresy.

The working group expresses its profound disappointment that the "white" churches continue to live as separate churches despite earlier calls by the LWF for the "white" churches in South Africa and Namibia to publicly and unequivocally denounce apartheid and to purge all vestiges of it from their institutions and life, and despite continued efforts of the other Lutheran churches in South Africa and in Namibia to dialog with these "white" churches and to form one fully united church with them. These churches therefore continue to affirm apartheid. They continue to participate actively in the violent dehumanization of people.

The Seventh Assembly RESOLVED:

10.1. To instruct the LWF Executive Committee to cooperate with the member churches in Namibia and in South Africa in providing all possible support to those individuals in the "white" churches who have worked and continue to work for positive change in their church bodies.

10.2. To urge the member churches to assist the people in South Africa to resist the "homelands" policy.

iii) Racism in the LWF and in the member churches

Because of the extreme violence of apartheid, which we as a working group have condemned as a heresy and for which the Assembly has suspended the "white" member churches in Namibia and in South Africa, all other member churches must be called on to cease all support of apartheid. To support institutions that support or condone apartheid is to participate in the sin of apartheid itself.

The Seventh Assembly RESOLVED:

10.3. To call upon those LWF member churches that provide financial and personnel support to the suspended "white" churches in Namibia and in South Africa, in consultation with other Lutheran churches in Namibia and in South Africa, to reconsider the agreements with these churches and either to suspend such support through an appropriate process or to find ways to assure that such support in no way assists those churches to continue to resist the change called for in the recommendation from the 1983 Pre-Assembly All Africa Lutheran Consultation in Harare, Zimbabwe, but rather assists them to be reconciled with their black brothers and sisters.

10.4. To ask the LWF member churches in the area as well as those supporting from the rest of the world to report annually to the LWF Executive Committee on progress toward these ends, and, should there be no positive movement on behalf of the "white" churches by January 1987, to request these supporting churches to terminate all financial and personnel support from that date on.

10.5. To urge the other LWF member churches in South Africa and Namibia to remember these suspended churches in their prayers, continuing to welcome their members and congregations into the fellowship of the Lutheran churches in Namibia and South Africa and offering to provide financial and personnel resources to those suspended churches as they are prepared to accept them.

10.6. To urge all LWF member churches to take visible and concrete steps, including boycott of goods and withdrawal of investments, to end all economic and cultural support of apartheid, even as they continue to urge their own governments, business organizations, and trade unions to observe strict enforcement of military and oil embargoes and boycotts concerning culture, sports, the transfer of nuclear technology, and the importation of nuclear materials in order to isolate and cut off South Africa until such time as apartheid is totally dismantled.

10.7. To ask each LWF member church to actively oppose all forms of racism in its own life and in the life of each country, particularly as this is expressed in times of growing unemployment and economic concern, especially against foreign workers, ethnic minorities, and refugees.

10.8. To ask each LWF member church to take action to remove all vestiges of institutional racism from their structures, reporting to the LWF Executive Committee on these efforts by January 1988 in order that these reports can be shared with the other member churches for their edification and prayerful support.

10.9. To refer to the Executive Committee for consideration that, in electing new members to commissions and new commission chairpersons, it be assured that the elected persons are always the ones with the best qualifications for the task, and that churches from the "South" are represented in each commission and among the chairpersons of each commission by a percentage at least equal to their membership in the LWF.

The Seventh Assembly further RESOLVED:

10.10. To adopt the following statement:
We, like our societies, are infected with racism, and therefore the LWF and each of our churches carries the disease of racism. We confess the sin of racism. We repent for the harm it continues to inflict on the lives of people. We commit ourselves to change. We call on our churches to examine their lives, to repent of their sins of racism, and to take action to reform their lives.

Sermon on Table Mountain

Blessed are the poor in apartheid votes,
for theirs is the nonracial future.

Blessed are those who mourn in Pollsmoor,
for freedom shall wipe away their tears.

Blessed are gentle prisoners in Robben Island,
for their isolation shall bring many together.

Blessed are those who hunger and thirst for justice,
for they will heal our broken nation.

Blessed are those who show mercy to apartheid victims,
for they give hope to many.

Blessed are those whose hearts are purified of racism,
for racists have no abode in the father's house.

Blessed are the freedom fighters,
for they will bring peace to all.

Blessed are the life prisoners,
those persecuted for their color,
for the kingdom of democracy is theirs.

Blessed are you when racists insult you,
And ban you,
And call you all names,
On account of your love for justice.

Jump up and shout *amandla*,
for your day of freedom is near,
for so racists persecuted Mugabe and Kaunda before you.

You are the liberators of the land;
if liberators sell out,
who will rehabilitate them?
They are puppets,
good for the garbage bin,
and ridiculed by their own people.

You are freedom signs of the oppressed.
Freedom fighters cannot be trounced.

Nor do democrats light the flame
And smother it under the ego;
they hoist it like a flag,
calling on the oppressed to stand up.

Let your freedom zeal dwarf all oppression,
So that the downtrodden may see the path to Uhuru;
And glorify God and his freedom children.

Do not think that freedom destroys law and order.
It does not destabilize;
it creates justice and peace.

Until apartheid and racism pass away,
not the youngest child will give up the struggle,
not until the evil is uprooted—trunk, root, and all.

Whoever robs one of these blacks of the least of his human
  rights,
And teaches that apartheid is from God,
he shall be called heretic in the kingdom of God.
Whoever respects these rights and promotes them,
he shall be called liberator in the kingdom of God.

Unless your nonracialism surpasses that of Hitler and
  Verwoerd,
You are no material for eternal life.

You have heard the Immorality Act say:
You shall not love across the color bar,
Who ever so loves falls foul of the law.

But I say to you:
If you frown at your neighbor's color,
You frown at his maker.
If you shout "kaffir" at your compatriot,
You roll his maker in the mud.
If you expose his mind to "Bantu education,"
You insult his maker's brain.

If you are kneeling for sacraments in the *kerk*,[1]
And remember that Mandela is still in prison,
turn your back on the chalice,
first open the prison door,
reconcile yourself to Winnie his wife,
then go back and recite "*Ons vader in die hemel.*"[2]

1. *kerk:* church.
2. Our Father who art in heaven.

Make friends with the oppressed while still on the way to
freedom,
Lest you curse your color on freedom day,
And reap the fruits of the Internal Security Act,
drinking to the last poison drop from the apartheid cup.

You have heard the Prohibition of Mixed Marriages Act say:
In one bed black and white is adultery,
even if blessed by pope.
But I say to you:
Every dominie[3] taking a black nanny to Lesotho,
to impose his holiness upon her black chastity,
his throne is not among the saints.

And if the right wing pulls you to Waterberg,[4]
tear it out and throw away the malignant tumor.
It is better for a few racists to commit suicide
than for the whole of Afrikanerdom to be thrown into hell.

If the ultra-right wing pulls you to Morass-stad,
cut Marais out and right the wrong.
It is better to sacrifice cheap unity for eternal life
than plunge into hell hand in hand.

You heard Influx Control say:
Whoever sends back to the homeland an exhausted Bantu,
Let him give him a certificate of "out of order."

But I say to you:
Whoever exploits my children,
And calls them expendable labor,
reduces them to animals,

3. dominie: reverend.

4. Waterberg: ultraconservative constituency in the Transvaal province of South Africa.

And whoever marries this evil,
marries my wrath.

At Blood River you heard it said:
God's covenants are not enough,
Afrikaner make your own.

But I say to you:
Create no racist covenants,
either at the Voortrekker monument,
or at Verwoerd's tomb,
for all these are God's places of justice,
God's shrines of equality.

Do not swear by "Die Stem,"
for it is the anthem of hate;
or by the Republic,
for it is a symbol of exclusion;
nor by your head,
for you are heading for trouble.

Let your development be development,
not parallel development;
Let your white be white,
God did not create Adam and honorary Adam.
All these qualifications racist minds produce.

You have heard it said:
"Dit sal die dag weers,"[5]
Kaffir will know his place.

But I say to you:
Walk not into racial slogans.
When you are incited against God,
Let agitator jump first into the ring,
You have no cheek to serve as a punching bag.

And whoever shall force you back to the homeland,
force him back to Holland too.

Give to him who asks for trouble,
And do not turn away from him until he asks for mercy.

You have heard it said:
You shall love only whites
And hate blacks.

But I say to you:
Love blacks too.

And you blacks, pray for those who persecute you,
So that you may live as freely as your father,
to share his graces:
basking in his colorless sun,
his colorless rain drenching the colorful earth.

For if you love within your race,
What inbreeding is that?
Does Satan not love himself?

And if you greet your sisters only,
How do you better the record of whitehead?
Did the Nazis not do better?

Christian sisters,
Christian brothers,
Muslims and Hindus,
Buddhists and traditionalists,
  Atheists,
  Neutralists,
You have heard it said:

5. Afrikaans for "over my dead body."

Condemn apartheid, yet trade with it,
Call for its end, yet veto resolutions to end it,
Condemn white violence and also black resistance,
Deny blacks support and condemn those who offer it;
  Move in circles till you "become a wheel,"
  Wallow in mud till you become a pig,
  Repeat a lie till it's iced with truth,
  Vilify the truth till it sounds like a lie,
  Call Satan God till he speaks in tongues,
  Call heaven hell till flames leap on angels' wings.
    "If only Christian nations were nations of Christians."
    If faith were not only a domesticated mamba,
    It would bite and evil would perish,
    Sermon on Mount Pretoria.

11

Through a Minefield of Plots and Traps

When any government enacts a law, it is a law. Those who obey it are law-abiding citizens, and those who disobey it are criminals. People like me boast of a conviction-free record under the South African laws. Is this a plus or a minus? Can one obey these laws and still be obedient to God? I doubt it. Perhaps all of us who have clean records have reason to seek absolution. Perhaps we have been saved by too much caution or half-hearted commitment. Or double standards, chasing with the hounds and running with the hares. Perhaps we are just empty gongs making a lot of noise, mere political irritants to Pretoria, ineffective in our strategies. Now and again we get a little attention from the police, a little harassment, a short detention here and another there, a banning order, a raid, a denial of passport. But are we really serious until we are charged, stand trial, and are convicted, or until such time as we deserve conviction?

On judgment day, will God not find us guilty of maintaining a guilt-free record under the laws of Satan? Will Mandela's record not be more respectable in heaven's court? In our earthly courts, previous convictions are a disadvantage; but who will have a clear conscience to stand before the judgment seat of history, and of the Almighty, and boast: "I lived for forty (or fifty, or sixty . . . or a hundred) years in South Africa. I was never charged. Never tried. Never convicted." Will such innocents not be found guilty of the sin of omission? Or of collaboration as silent accomplices? Or of lack of commitment? Or of lack of dedicated service? Or of lack of desire to uphold the truth? Or of evasiveness instead of taking a stand? Guilty of not being guilty where guilt is required?

The prophets were often charged, tried, convicted, and executed. So was Christ. The apostles. The reformers. And many more after them. Why is it so difficult for South Africa's satanic police and courts to charge, try, and convict us? Execute us? I can only hope that it is not because we are neither hot nor cold. Perhaps it is through God's loving grace and the sustaining prayers of the saints. But on the other hand, if we are ineffective, why does Satan work day and night to entrap us, to plot against us? Prophets faced traps and plots. So did Christ. So did the apostles after him. Today we face the same old Satan.

Show me the way.

A policeman's son (I shall call him Bill) led a group of young students to a pastor's home.

Bill: We are tired of Bantu education. Good prophet, only you can help us. You know the truth, the way, and the life. Take us, show us the way to Botswana.

Pastor: I have never been to Botswana. You will have to try elsewhere.

Synthesis: Later, they were all "arrested" at the border, except for Bill: he had not gone with them. Some, apparently unwilling participants in the plot, were pressured to implicate the pastor in an attempt to recruit students for banned organizations. When this failed, all were released, uncharged. During three of his four detentions, the pastor faced questions on this matter. In a petition organized by some top government civil servants, this matter came up:

SECRET

P. O. Sibasa
REPUBLIC OF VENDA
17/02/86

The Right Reverend Bishop Serote
Evangelical Lutheran Church in
South Africa: Northern Diocese
P. O. Box 1186
Pietersburg
0700

We have for ten years watched with dismay how our church leaders got themselves entangled in activities that discredited and tarnished the good name of the Lutheran Church.

For ten years we remained silent hoping that things would improve, but alas, we are getting from bad to worse. We are prepared to serve our God without being dragged into unending clashes with the Governments and authorities of the land. We live in Venda and we practise our Christianity in Venda; and we feel that the revolutionary activities of our Deans and Pastors will lead us nowhere.

In 1977 some boys who skipped the country to be trained as terrorists abroad were assembled at Beuster Church Centre. In 1980 the terrorists who bombed the Sibasa Police Station, killing two policemen, were given accommodation at Beuster Church Centre and were also transported from there by a vehicle belonging to the Church Centre.

Quite recently on 31 January 1986, Beuster was under siege of police force because a meeting was to be held at the Church Centre on 01 February 1986. The question we ask ourselves is how on earth can another person choose my home as a venue for his meeting without my knowledge? Before the appointment of Dean T. S. Farisani, and Pastor Phosiwa, Beuster was a peaceful place and people used to pray to their God happily. We have no peace of mind and we do not wish to be identified with the activities of these leaders of our church.

We want the Church to go on as it has been doing even before the present dean and pastors came into the picture. What we abhor is that our church should be used as a launching pad of terrorist attacks on Government buildings and institutions. The substantial sums of moneys that we pay to the Church come from the very Government that our Church leaders say we should break ties with. The same Mahosi described as puppets of P. W. Botha in the pamphlets distributed in Venda were the Mahosi who gave pieces of land to the early missionaries; the very pieces of land the church calls its own today.

We find it difficult to attend any meeting that the dean and pastors call, for we do not want to align ourselves with their underground activities. The members of the Lutheran Church in Venda are upset about the underground activities of our dean and some pastors, and for the sake of the life of the church you have to do something as Bishop in charge of this area.

We request you, Right Reverend Bishop, to transfer the very Dean T. S. Farisani, Pastor Phosiwa and pastor Nevhutalu to some places outside Venda not later than 31 March 1986.

We know that this will be a difficult and painful action to take, but for the sake of thousands of people who want to see their church prospering and for the avoidance of any split in the church it will be right for you to take such action.

This decision was arrived at as a result of a meeting held at Makwarela Hall on the 12 February 1986 by members of the Lutheran Church in Venda. It was further agreed at that meeting that if this request cannot be granted, the Lutherans in Venda will be left with no option but to take an unpleasant alternative such as stopping to make any financial contributions for instance. This is not meant to be a threat to the Church, but to show how the people are prepared to have this thorn out of the neck as it is painful.

YOURS IN CHRIST. . . .

Show me the way, give me the cash.

He spoke Venda, he came from Johannesburg, or so he said. I shall call him Judas.
Judas: I need help. I need cash. And the way to Botswana.
Pastor: Who are you?
Judas: I am Venda. I was expelled from Morris Isaacson High School. I was working. My father ate up my money. I got four hundred rand a month.
Pastor: What is your name?
Judas: Help me.
Pastor: Is your name Help Me? How do you know me?
Judas: You are the great lion of the north. We all know you. You are our hero, our leader.
Pastor: Botswana is nearer when you are in Johannesburg. Why do you come here, far away from your intended destination?
Judas: For guidance.
Pastor: I have neither cash nor guidance. Sorry, but you have to go.
Synthesis: Today all those who know him thank God for protecting his pastor.

Keep my explosive stuff, they are after me.

He came to live in Venda after years of life in Johannesburg. I shall call him Grill.
Grill: I am on the run. I have done things in Johannesburg. This record has Mandela's speech. Keep my banned books. I see you are active on this side too. Nineteen seventy-six will go down in

history as the year of freedom. How is the liberation struggle going here under your able guidance?
Pastor: We are chopping with the trusted two-edged sword. Congregations are overflowing. Apartheid is reeling under pressure.
Grill: I realize you have set the Boers' church at Tshilidzini on fire—and their many bookshops. Sentenced the apartheid evil structures to hell. Long live man of God! I wish we had many like you!
Pastor: I do not take credit for that. I do not know who did it and why.
Grill: Minor details will come later. Keep my stuff.
Synthesis: When police came a few days later, they turned the house upside down. They were, the pastor guessed, looking for the Mandela speech and the banned books. In his first and fourth detention, this matter came up prominently, even the matter of burnings. When the pastor was released, he said:
Pastor: Take back your books and record, Mr. Grill. Tell the police that your relative was listening to the record and reading the books when they came to arrest me.

Come let us eat together.

Now a resident in a makeshift wood house, he invited one black pastor and one white pastor to have lunch in his house during a break in the three-day human rights conference. I shall call him, again, Mr. Grill.
Grill: Now you are the greatest prophet who has ever emerged in Afrikanerdom. Can you really tell me how you started, how and why you broke away from the broederbond, what you do now in the liberation struggle? The power of God must surely dwell in you.
Black Pastor: It is not easy for me to talk about myself. As for my background and activities, I have shared this last night and today. More will come this afternoon and tomorrow morning. Will you be there?

Grill: Yes, but I wanted something deeper, something more active, more direct, something that can inspire me to action and if . . .
Synthesis: Grill's recording gadgets misfired for a split second, the pastors heard, but did not know whether he knew that they knew. The next day, before the Sunday service, police came to tell the Afrikaner pastor that he had no right to be at a black church center without a permit. God won, and the pastor preached.

We know, but help us to understand our choices.

They were two young Venda boys, probably around sixteen years old. I shall call them Twins (whereas one spoke more than the other, I shall have them speak together).
Twins: We are freedom fighters. We want you to help us choose our targets.
Pastor: Who sent you?
Twins: The ANC.
Pastor: To me?
Twins: Yes.
Pastor: The ANC should know that I know nothing about targets. You probably misheard and misunderstood your instructions.
Twins: Please help. Please help!
Pastor: I cannot even help myself choose a target, except for the gospel. Sorry, I cannot help.
Synthesis: When in his third detention, the pastor saw the twins in the employ of the system. They mocked him as he lay naked in the water, handcuffed behind the back.

Even on the run, people shall share.

Several pastors had gathered at Motetema in late 1981 for an ordination retreat. At one public resort, a young man approached one of them. I shall call him Refugee.
Refugee: Power, brother. I am from Wits University. They are

after me. I am here now, helping my brother in his business. Before you leave, I shall bring you lots of relevant literature to take home to promote the struggle.

Pastor: How do you know me?

Refugee: Everybody knows you.

Synthesis: Next day, a beautiful young girl brought a pile of literature, hot political stuff, to where the pastor was. When the pastor left, he conveniently forgot the stuff where it had been brought to him. On the way home, his car was searched several times; clearly the police knew what they were looking for. Nothing certain can be said about this incident. Less than a month later the pastor was behind bars.

Is it not terrible?

When he heard about the death in detention of his friend, the pastor was more than a thousand kilometers from home. At two different places, two hundred kilometers apart, he was confronted by two different people, who said the same things. I shall call them Provocateurs.

Provocateurs: They have killed Isaac Muofhe. Only you can save the situation.

Pastor: How?

Provocateurs: Tit for tat and butter for fat.

Synthesis: In detention, police accused the prophet of planning tit for tat and butter for fat against them. It was false. Nothing is certain about the Provocateurs.

Thus says the Lord: Accommodate strangers.

The pastor had hardly been settled for fifteen minutes after his return from a three-month sick leave following almost seven months of torture-filled detention, when two young men came, with rucksacks on their backs. I shall call them Strangers.

Strangers: We are from two different countries in Scandinavia. Thohoyandou Hotel people have recommended that we come to you for accommodations. We want you to tell us about apartheid. Tomorrow we shall proceed to Zimbabwe.
Pastor: Keep your bags on the porch. Take your seats. Do you have visas or permits?
Strangers: No. Do we need them?
Synthesis: When the pastor was out consulting an elder prophet, his wife followed him.
Wife: The security police are at our house. They want you.
Captain White: How do you accommodate strangers without permits in your house? Come on. Carry them in your car to our office.
Pastor: I shall not carry your people for you. You do it yourself.
Synthesis: When they left, black policemen sat at the back of the truck, while Captain White sat with the two permitless strangers in front. Two or three weeks later, the pastor and his wife met someone who resembled one of the two strangers in the company of a known black security policeman. Both were speaking the local tongue. Nothing is certain about this incident.

S.O.S.

He calls himself different names at different times. He is black, but he speaks English all the time. I shall call him Mr. Broke.
Broke: I need immediate help—money. Car broken down . . . for projects . . . for other needs—please, now!
Pastor's wife: Who sent you?
Broke: SACC . . . no, Beyers . . . no, Manas . . . no, I do not know. Yes, I know . . . I shall phone . . . no, I do not have their numbers. You are a coward . . . a big coward. . . .
Broke: Hello, may I speak to the pastor?
Pastor: Hello, yes I am here . . .
Broke: I have delicate matters . . . may I come? . . . You know I cannot tell you on the phone. Will I find you?

Pastor: I am here, but I do not allow you to come.
Broke: I have a letter . . .
Pastor: I shall not read it.
Synthesis: Mr. Broke did this with many other anti-apartheid figures. At one Holiday Inn hotel, we saw him in the company of a girl whose connections with the system were known by all. I also came up behind him at a dry-cleaner's shop, where, unaware of my presence, he gave a different name and the local posh hotel as his address. He drove different expensive cars, including an Audi 5000. No one knows everything about this broken man.

You will see me but not know me: collision with ghosts.

When the pastor is not there, he comes; when the pastor appears, he disappears. When people are in bed, he flashes the torchlights; they can smell his tobacco. When they switch on the lights, he switches off his existence. When caught red-handed, he lies. When he gets a chance, he tries to cause artificial accidents for pastors and their wives, always disguised. He has no face and no mouth; we shall speak for him: Mr. Ghost.
Pastor: Who are you?
Ghost: Anonymous.
Pastor: What do you want around our house at night?
Ghost: Stolen cars. I was not there.
Pastor: Why do you run away from light?
Ghost: I am a child of darkness.
Pastor: Why do you want to smash into my wife's car and mine? Why do you interfere with our vehicles at night?
Ghost: If poisoning does not work, or is easily detectable, accidents are accidents. They work.
Pastor: When will you stop?
Ghost: Not till we have silenced God.
Pastor: Can you?
Ghost: This is not good diplomacy, not for us. You win public and diplomatic battles. Logical battles that depend on reasoned-

out arguments. We win secret ones. We have no ambition for public honors and U.N.O. medals. You speak the language of morals; we speak the language of gold and diamonds, the language of putting your mouth where your money is.
Pastor: How safe are we anywhere in the world then?
Ghost: We share everything.
Pastor: Even . . . ?
Ghost: You mean intelligence? Yes.
Pastor: On me?
Ghost: I shall not handle that one.
Synthesis: Life is a walk through a minefield of traps and plots, unless you follow the Great Minesweeper—God.
Ghost: We can. We have had some world powers silenced. In public, they are against us; behind the scenes they are with us. We are now busy working to silence God: blind him with tithes, long prayers, and anti-communism language.
Pastor: Can you name the powers?
Ghost: Are you joking?
Pastor: Yes—No! Their powers end where God's power begins. Amen.

Come, Let Us Sing Deadlock Music

For fifty years we spoke to a wide-eared dumb:
But in 1960 they silenced us,
  Charged us,
  Tried us,
  Convicted us,
  Shelved us.
  No talks anymore.

Eight years other vehicles were born:
But in 1977 they silenced nineteen,
  Charged us,
  Banned us,
  Banished us,
  Abolished us.
  No negotiations anymore.

Before long we were back again:
But they resorted to draconian measures against us,
  Charged us,
  Declared us affected,
  Labeled us infected by communism,
  Effaced us.
  No give and take between master and slave.

Then came the Committee for Conciliation:
But they sabotaged that too,
  Charged us,
  Disappointed us,
  Pushed us aside,
  Trampled us.
  No conference table with clever kaffirs.

Men and women of good will came together in Oxford:
But they mocked their every effort,

Charged us,
Mocked our intentions,
Resorted to *kragdadigheid*[1] arrogance,
Maligned us.
No more hobnobbing with terrorist sympathizers.

Came the Eminent Persons Group of the Commonwealth:
But you spat into their face,
Charged us,
Left Mugabe in shock,
Left Kaunda embarrassed,
Left Masire shattered.
No more talks that interfere with our domestic matters.

In pursuit of understanding, came the Long Island Harrison
Conference:
But they smothered every flame of hope,
Charged us,
Gave birth to a No Talks pamphlet of 70,000,
Defied sense and reason,
Detained black participants.
"Let these Bantu talk to the walls."

All roads lead to Lusaka in search of peace:
But they brought every stumbling block on the way,
Charged us,
Hounded us,
Harassed us,
Marooned us.
No more communication between citizen at home and
citizen in exile.

We brought back a message fresh and simple,
A message as old as the struggle:

1. *kragdadigheid:* hardheaded, tough-handed.

If they will let political prisoners go free,
If they will let exiles back home,
If they will withdraw troops from black areas,
If they will lift the state of emergency,

If they will repeal apartheid laws,
If they will genuinely dismantle apartheid,
And agree to a ceasefire,
And accept a majority government,
In one undivided, nonracial South Africa,
Where democracy will be the order of the day—

Then we shall:
Then we shall lay down our arms,
Then we shall process the people's will,
Then we shall consult the ballot box,
Then Mthembu and Malan shall vote side by side,
Replacing appointees with the people's choice,
And our country shall know peace again.

We carry a precious message for the church:
Go home and find an alternative,
An effective way to end apartheid.
If that works, we shall join you,
For we use not violence for violence' sake.
If you have no effective alternative,
Do not call us to prayer when the other side shoots.
If you have no effective alternative,
Do not condemn our only effective means.
Guns are guns and they kill,
Whether of British or Soviet origin.
That is not the point.
They have chaplains and we have ours,
They do not shoot before they pray,
Our guns are blessed too.

We shall not fire the last bullet,
But we shall not stop till they stop.
When blacks die, there's no talk of civilians killed,
When whites die, civilians are killed,
And yet we know every white is a soldier,
At eighteen they are marksmen—and -women,
Now they are training children.
We wish we had a choice,
But we do not.

We brought a message for those in usurped power:
If they want to talk, the mouth is above the chin;
If they want to listen, the ears are above the jaws.
If they want to see, the two balls are called eyes;
If they want to reason, the box is above the shoulders,
If they want people to talk to:
The island is within their reach,
Pollsmoor below their Table Mountain Resort.
The prisons are bulging at the seams,
Full of minds and brains that do not belong there.
On trial every day, from coast to coast,
Are men and women whose wit is above the bench that sits
   in judgment.
Scattered on the face of the earth
Are sons and daughters whose word is echoed within
Their kith and kin inside South Africa.
The poverty is one of will,
Not of skillful visionaries at the conference table.

Tshenuwani in Monologue

Tshenuwani I: Who are we in white theology? It is not always easy to distinguish between official white theology and white street theology, just as it is very difficult, almost impossible, to distinguish between apartheid the ideology and apartheid the theology. Nowhere is this unholy marriage better defined than in the saying: the Dutch Reformed churches are the Nationalist party at prayer, while the Nationalist party is the Dutch Reformed churches at politics. To understand the place of black people in white theology, one needs to go beyond official church documents and public declarations and resolutions. Their proper exegesis is done at their homes, at work, in the street, in their jokes, in their speeches, in their actions, in their attitudes, in their sermons, in their politics, in their lifestyle. Actions speak louder than words. Who is the so-called bantu (in small letters) in God's scheme of things? Since 1652, especially after the so-called "Great Trek" of the early nineteenth century, and particularly since 1948, the fateful year when the Afrikaner Nationalist Party wrested power from Jan Smuts' United Party in a surprise election victory, white—especially Dutch Reformed—theology has occasionally taken its cue from rank and file as well as government beliefs, and vice versa.

Tshenuwani II: The Dutch Reformed Church, and whites in general, will protest against this observation. However, their mild protest or lack of protest against Afrikaner street theology—also their very own theology at the level of praxis—is enough evidence that baboon creation and performance theology was not only tolerated but encouraged and accommodated in the holy of holies. At least that is the black experience, and indeed my own personal experience as one of the apes. I am taking you on the highway of black experience. Depending on your endurance and pace, it goes on . . . and on . . . and on.

IV

TSHENUWANI'S FOURTH TIME IN THE BOWELS OF HELL

12

The Siege

A day or two earlier, my wife Regina had had a dream of police surrounding our church house. At about eleven o'clock on the night of November 21, 1986, her dream materialized with the familiar knock on the door. When the knocks spread to every door and to the windows, we knew that the days of peaceful sleep were over. As torches flashed from window to window, we could hear heavy and light footsteps around the house. We suspected that vigilantes had come to solve the Farisani problem once and for all. They banged the doors and the windows, and every bang was like a spear piercing through the heart. We peeked through the curtains and saw unrecognizable figures in human form, one of whom—given the limits of poor visibility—was dressed like a pastor and had a Bible-like book in his hand. As the knocks continued, they began to call out my name: "Open! Open, Dean Farisani! You have visitors. We are your guests." Bang, bang, bang! Bang, bang, bang! "Open, man! We say open, man! Open!"

For a moment there was some calm, and we heard them opening the garage doors. "They are opening your garage," my mother whispered into our bedroom. Fearing that speech could betray us, we whispered back: "Shhh. Shhh. Please go back to your room." When they saw that both personal and church vehicles were in, they knew that their prey was in the lair. They moved from room to room on the outside shining the flashlights through the windows. Our thick, somewhat opaque curtains did not make their task very easy. When they came to our bedroom, we were already lying on the floor, in case a volley of bullets burst directly at our bed. We had dressed up for any eventuality.

When they started battling the front door, I crawled to the phone, which had been extended to our bedroom some time before, and contacted Dr. Daniel Tavenier at Donald Fraser Hospital, some twenty kilometers away. I phoned relatives and friends at Sibasa, Johannesburg, and Vereeniging, as well as the secretary general of the South African Council of Churches, Dr. Beyers Naudé, and Mervin Assur, our church general secretary. I tried a pastor's number in London and got it wrong. I gave them the name, John Evenson, hoping that this would help trace his number—without success. By this time they had broken into the house, and the lounge and passage had become occupied territory. To reach my office, where the telephone directories were kept, I would have to pass through the part of my house that had fallen into enemy hands. I cracked my brain to remember telephone numbers of friends in Africa, Europe, and the United States. None came. Just before I collapsed in frustration, one number flashed past my mind, that of Hanna and Wilhelm Steffens in Hermannsburg, West Germany. They were absent, but somebody promised to pass on the message. Another flash brought another number, and this time we were lucky: Superintendent Hans-Wilhelm Hube, our German partner dean, got our S.O.S. call. By this time they—for up to now the intruders were only "they," unannounced, unintroduced—were battling to force open our bedroom door. Apparently the bent lock was a hard nut to crack, because their attempts to break the lock were punctuated by pleas that we open the door. By this time all of the children were crying, while my mother lectured the unannounced guests, and my nephew was praying for the earth to open up and swallow him—if it would not cave in under the intruders. If they had known about our bedroom telephone, they surely would have cut the line!

"Who are you and what do you want here?" It was the welcome voice of Dr. Tavenier challenging the unsuspecting "they." It was too good to be true. Not that he and his doctor colleague, Zomerdijk, both from the Netherlands, could save us. But now we knew that, whatever happened, we would not die in obscurity or just disappear without a trace, as many opponents of apartheid had disappeared before.

"We are police and we want the dean."

For the first time we knew who they were, and I burst out: "Why do you come at midnight? I travel openly during the day. Why don't you arrest me in daytime?"

"Open, Dean, we do not want to arrest you," they countered very feebly.

"I shall not open to murderers and torturers. Do you remember what you did to me during my third detention? I still have scars on my kneecaps, wrists, and elbows—all over my body. You are murderers. Go, call Mr. Botha and Mr. Mphephu to come here. I shall talk to them, not you."

"Open, Dean. Those are things of the past; we are not coming for that. We can assure you."

"That is what you say here in front of people. Lies of torturers and murderers. There they are: all those murderers and torturers have been promoted. I shall not open for you at night. If you want me, you will have to wait for the morning."

The two doctors assured me that they would stay in the house until morning, to see what would happen to me.

"Open, Dean, please, please, please! Do not stretch our patience too far."

Bang, bang, bang.

"I shall not open for you at night. You broke the front door. Why don't you break all the other doors? Why don't you shoot your way into the bedroom. What are your guns for? I am tired of persecutions by Satan and his angels. Tired. Tired. Tired."

"Who opened for you?"

Dr. Zomerdijk confronted them further.

"Whose house is this? Is it your house?"

"You keep quiet. We are doing our job. This is the law. We are police. We know our work."

"What work?" I asked. "What is it that you know? Moving around at night and breaking into church houses when people are sleeping? Torturing and killing innocent people, that is all you know! Where is Isaac Muofhe? Where is Solomon Tshikhudo? Why did I spend 106 days in a hospital in 1982?" I wanted to tell them a piece of my mind before I died.

By now telephone calls were coming in like a heavy downpour: from Sibasa and Thohoyandou, from Johannesburg and the Vaal Triangle, and from West Germany. We had thrown caution to the winds, and were conversing as loudly as we could. They were probably listening to and recording all the conversations; but why they did not cut the telephone line is still a mystery. When I got tired of throwing direct verbal missiles at the police through the solid door, and indirect ones in my telephone conversations, I fell on the bed and slept, while Regina handled the phone calls. "They" had given up on the door. Outside, we could hear people singing and praying, as if to wake a God who was oblivious to the waves tossing the boat in which he slept:

> *Khosi dumbu ndi lihulu* (Father, the storm is heavy)
> *Na muya a u bvumaho* (and the roaring wind)
> *Ri tshidze vhona ri a lovha* (Save us, look we die),
> *Hu kona henewe* (Only you are able).
> *Hee madumbu na lwanzhe ipfani-ha* (Listen storms and sea),
> *Ndi tshi kaidza ni fhumule* (When I reprimand, be silent)
> *Ni tshete ni tshete* (Be dead calm, dead calm).

At the end of my short nap, reality stared me in the eye: it was not a nightmare; the police were still there. They were there for Dean Tshenuwani Simon Farisani, and they would not leave without their prey with a price on his head. I also needed to go to the toilet. I held back, but when the bladder threatened to burst open, I made for the window. I wanted to open it and let rain through the burglar proofs. If the police were in the way, bad luck; if they shot, well, that's it. From nowhere my wife brought a hot-water bottle, long emptied and forgotten after the winter cold. It did not take long to fill, for by now my bladder had become hyperactive.

When dawn broke, I dressed properly, putting on my clerical shirt and collar, and my white gown. We read the Bible, as we had done most of the night, and we prayed. I phoned Beyers Naudé, Pastor Phaswana, our executive secretary, and my brother-in-law:

"The hour has come for me to be dragged away again. My former torturers are here, among others. I am now handing myself over. Many thanks for your prayers and support throughout the long night—the longest night of my life." I dropped the phone, opened the door, walked past a security policeman posted at the toilet door, and entered the lounge. I did not expect to find the two doctors in the lounge. Mother had already told us that they had been arrested at five that morning. It was now half-past six.

They handed me a warrant of arrest, which I had demanded in vain throughout the night, but they had refused to push it under the door. With the exception of the second detention, the other two arrests had come without warrants. This one was in Afrikaans, and I read it loudly to my family, translating it into Venda: I was arrested under state security laws, indefinitely. . . . I was not to be allowed visitors . . . or books . . . or food. It was signed by the brigadier of the security police, who once responded when challenged by my wife after my 1982 tortures: "But we have paid your husband." My wife had struck back then: "Blood money! We have not used a single cent. All is going to church projects."

I visited the toilet, then went into the bedroom with my wife and got a toiletry bag. I could read the growing impatience on their faces, and their leader gave vent to his pent-up frustration, but not without self-control: "You keep on going back to the bedroom . . . only toiletry is allowed . . . no Bible or . . . you know that . . . let us go."

As I led them out of the house in my full clerical gear, shining silver cross on my chest pointing the way, I felt like a cornered sheep leading a pack of wolves from the safety of the kraal, into the bush where mutton needs no advertising. Now outside, for the first time I appreciated the intensity of the operation: police and soldiers were all over—walking around the house, on the lawn, in the flowers, lying on their bellies, perched in trees, on the premises, and with R1 and R2 military rifles at the ready, while security police, strutting like peacocks among them, wore faces and clothes of innocence, below which were hidden pistols and revolvers that rhythmically grinned with the to-and-fro movements of the hip bones. When I saw all this, I knew I was innocent.

After kissing my wife and three children, I embraced my mother and broke into song: *Phalaphala,* Hymn number 2:

Ndi tshi vhong muphulusi (When I see the Savior),
A tshi fa tshifhambanoni (Dying on the cross),
Ndi a lata zwa shangoni (I abandon worldly things),
U dihudza na vhutshinyi (Pride and sin).
Ndi nga si tsha tama tshithu (I will not chase after anything)
Tsho fhambanaho na Yesu (Contrary to Jesus' will);
Zwine ene a zwi funa (What he likes),
Nne-vho ndi a mu nekedza (That I dedicate to him).
Vhonani-ha thoho yawe (Look at his head),
Zwanda zwawe na milenzhe (His hands, and his feet)!
Vho mu vhambela kha thanda (They nailed him to a tree)—
Zwi na vhutungu vhuhulu (What terrible pain)!
Ndi nga isa mini khae (What shall I take to him)
Tshi konaho U mu renda (That is worthy to praise him)?
A thi na tsho fanelaho (I have nothing worthy),
Ndi do mu nekedza mbilu (I shall give him my heart).

I sat in the back, between two security police. Sergeant Smart Smile sat behind the wheel.

"This man before me, Captain Above-the-Law, is one of my 1982 torturers," I said out the car window to my mother and wife and children in Venda. As we passed the church building on the right, on our left pastors and congregants were seated on the grass, some singing, some in prayer, some doing only God knows what. They were prevented from entering the premises, let alone the house. From this vantage point they could see part of my house, and, as now, they would see me go. I waved to Pastor Theo Dau, my deputy, but his eyes were fixed on the sky above. I waved to pastor Zwo C. Nevhutalu, but his eyes were closed and his hands were clasped on his long legs; his trembling lips reminded me of childless Hanna's prayer.

And then, like a bolt from the blue:

"What were you saying to your wife about Me? Who does not know Me? Do you have to introduce Me? You are going to dig up all the guns you have on your premises. This time we shall close your mouth once and for all. *Nyẹmianu!*"[1]

This was the sergeant I had known, always above the law, now promoted to Captain Above-the-Law.

"Do what you like," I said. "The guns you buried on my premises you will dig out yourself. You also know that you tortured me. I talk about it. I write about it. I am willing to die for it. You tortured me."

They all laughed, except Captain Above-the-Law. In total silence we drove up the gravel road, turned to the right at Ngovhela, past the torture center, to the Sibasa police station, seven kilometers from my home.

Then I thought about my mother, as I do now.

Mother Love

Your person—
    short and tough
    ready and prepared
    for days and ways ahead.
True to your form—
    thorough of thought
    thorough bred
    royal blood in your veins.

Your courage—
    as you work in the fields
    removing the weeds between the seeds
    to feed strangers and kith and kin.
Tuned to your nature—
    fierce and fiery in the sun
    calm and tranquil in the cold
    freedom streams in your bones.

1. *Nyemianu:* scolding insult meaning "Your mother's private parts!"

Your firm stand—
As you discipline a son and daughters five
Facing dad in his boots
Confounding me with my books.
Towed by hands of time—
Stood your ground among women
Firmed your lips before the gods
Changed your faith in the face of all.

Your durability—
assailed by disease of ill degree
pushed and pulled from side to side
dragged and drubbed by man and nature.
Tunneled by trial and temptation—
You emerged strong with scars of sorrow
Valleys of sleepless nights cut on your face
Facing the unknown unfold without gold

Your sacrifice—
as four times I was dragged before your face
four times as sonless as you came
four times your life in exchange
for only son in grip of death.
Tied to your words—
"Run me over to cover my tears
Push me down to drown my sorrows
Let me die and not my son
Kill me first before my son."

Your prayer life—
All songs on your twisted lips
Commandments at your beck and call
Moving library of Bible stories
Dwarfing the tallest among professors.
Tailing Christ all the way—
Mocked for Christ and beaten for Jesus

Undressed for faith and starved for the cross
Persecuted by fate and institution
Crawling on and on the *via dolorosa.*

Your love for the neighbor—
No woman of the cloth
You clothed the naked
No woman of letters
You counseled professors.
Your willingness to share—
Sharing something when you had none
Giving all when you had some
A better pastor I've not met
You shame the rich and enrich the poor.

Your patience robust and round—
As we all leave you alone and old
As your only son you see no more,
Daughter-in-law and grandchildren three,
Detained by distance beyond the pale.
If you die alone and broke—
As we linger along foreign coasts,
Know one thing I've not told:
Your will-of-love, longer than life,
We'll pass on to generations unborn.

13

Before I Opened My Mouth

At the Sibasa police station, I sat on a trunk tin in my gown. I played with my cross and felt very happy. The saying is true: Joy is not the absence of suffering but the presence of the Lord. When they came to me, there was nothing new. They recycled the old tired issues of procedure: watch, belt, money, and books, if any—and I had no books—I was to leave in the safe custody of the police. And I got a receipt. All the police were very polite and considerate.

Cell No. 5 had apparently been prepared in a hurry that morning. The toilets and face basin were oily with dirt, and there were patches of water all over the floor. Dead mosquitoes were floating freely in their eternal sleep, while the living had very good reason not to die before the start of that night's festive season. Bedding? No change since my stay here in 1977 and again in 1982. Furniture? Nothing. Outside view? A void of nothingness. The toilet in the shower cubicle functioned, but not the one in the cell. Soap and toilet paper? Plenty, unlike in my past visits. And also a door between the cell and a wall-enclosed court was never locked, unlike in the past. The two mesh-wire windows—one at the back and one in front, heavily reinforced with steel bars—brought in enough light, by previous comparisons, more light, if the middle door remained open.

From inside the cell, it was impossible to see anything outside, more a disadvantage of height—or rather, lack of it—on my part. But it was possible to hear people speaking outside, and if

I spoke loudly enough, they could also hear me. From the shower court, through crossed steel bars, I could see the blue sky and, occasionally, a lonely black cloud wandering aimlessly in space. On top of the tall friendly tree that towered over the cell, two crows sat every evening, in white clerical collars and black gowns, merging their music with mine:

O Lord my God, when I in awesome wonder
Consider all the works thy hand hath made,
I see the stars, I hear the rolling thunder,
Thy pow'r throughout the universe displayed:
Then sings my soul, my savior God to thee,
How great thou art! How great thou art!
Then sings my soul, my savior God to thee,
How great thou art! How great thou art!

When through the woods and forest glades I wander,
I hear the birds sing sweetly in the trees;
When I look down from lofty mountain grandeur
And hear the brook and feel the gentle breeze:
Then sings my soul, my savior God to thee,
How great thou art! How great thou art!
Then sings my soul, my savior God to thee,
How great thou art! How great thou art!

But when I think that God, his son not sparing,
Sent him to die, I scarce can take it in,
That on the cross my burden gladly bearing
He bled and died to take away my sin;
Then sings my soul, my savior God to thee,
How great thou art! How great thou art!
Then sings my soul, my savior God to thee,
How great thou art! How great thou art!

When Christ shall come, with shouts of acclamation,
And take me home, what joy shall fill my heart!
Then I shall bow in humble adoration
And then proclaim, "My God how great thou art!"

Then sings my soul, my savior God to thee,
How great thou art! How great thou art!
Then sings my soul, my savior God to thee,
How great thou art! How great thou art![1]

It sounded and felt like a pastors' convention at evening devotions: Crows and man in praise of God!

I sat on the floor and prayed, and when I said amen, Captain Above-the-Law stood at the door and asked me what the hell was going on in my mind. I told him the hell in my mind:

"I shall not speak to murderers and torturers. I sued you, I wrote about you; your story is in video, and if I live, I shall continue to expose your atrocities. I expect no fairness and objectivity from you. How can my torturers be my investigators, interrogators, and judges?"

He stood tall, fierce but defeated, and as he walked away he mumbled something like "*Vha amba hani, Vho-Dean naa?* (How do you speak, Dean?)." But he did not wait for my response.

"You asked for it. To them that ask it shall be given."

He probably got half the dose, for before I closed my mouth, the door closed between us; and a split second before that, he had closed his mind.

When lunch came, I refused to eat: I am no criminal and therefore no candidate for their ill-prepared hard porridge or *phuthu*, served with oversalted *kupugani*[2] gravy. They left it in the cell, and after one hour collected it.

In late afternoon I found myself being driven away by three security police, huddled in the back of a canopied yellow police truck in my clerical gown. This was it, I thought. Not yet. I ended up at Tshilidzini hospital, where Doctor Zöllner did a thorough medical checkup and noted down all the scars on my body and limbs, most of which had their origins in my first and third detentions. How much I wished he could note the scars on my

1. Lutheran Book of Worship, Hymn 532.
2. *kupugani:* "get healed" gravy, used mainly for poor, malnourished children.

mind! He declared me fit but demanded to see me the following Monday to check my heart condition, which caused him some concern. He gave Sergeant Blacknut a note to the division commander, who had presided over my torture on January 5, 1982.

I had hoped that the doctor would consult me in private, not in the presence of the police. Faced with no safer choice, I took the plunge, to the shock of the police:

"Previously I was tortured very badly. You have my records in this hospital. You have seen the scars. This very morning I was threatened with death. If I do not honor the Monday appointment, or any other appointments thereafter, you can safely guess at the reasons."

The doctor nodded and emphasized that it was vital that I keep the appointment.

I dressed and we left. Since the truck canopy was covered with canvas cloth, I could not see outside and never knew where I was at any given moment. The ten-kilometer stretch is a built-up area, but our truck traveled well above the 60-kph speed limit, at times hovering around 100 kph. A traffic officer caught us in a speed trap. But Blacknut looked into his face, the officer apologized, and we shot away. What power can restrain these people? I asked myself and folded up.

When supper came, I did not eat. I am no criminal, and therefore no candidate for their monotonous lunch and supper: *phuthu* and *kupugani* gravy. The only difference between lunch and supper was in temperature: lunch was steaming hot, supper was on the cool to cold side.

I had brought a pair of shoes, socks, pants, and underpants, one undershirt, one clerical shirt, a white collar, my gown and cross. The prickly dirty blankets were as unaccommodating as ever; so after prayer, I chose to sleep in my clothes.

I refused to eat Sunday morning breakfast. I am no criminal, and no candidate for their oversugared soft porridge for which there is no spoon. Unless I was given food fit for human consumption, or allowed to use my fifty rand in police custody, or received food from home, I would refuse to eat until death. For my Sunday holy communion, I used a piece of their porridge and water.

Who could believe it? Between late September and mid-November, I had been globe-trotting: Britain, U.S.A., Switzerland, West Germany, Zambia. But now here I was: from five-star hotels to five stars below the sty-accommodation in a dungeon of cruelty!

Who believed me? After my internationally publicized third detention and the civil suit that the government settled out of court, people all over the world were saying: "With his new-found status, the dean is now immune from police action. After the embarrassing and widely publicized tortures and lawsuits, the government has learned its lesson." They laughed at me when I refused to speak of my third detention as my last detention, dismissing it as part of my nature that underplays things. I did then, as I do now, assert: Apartheid and repressive measures, with all accompanying tortures and murders, are two inseparable Siamese twins: you can't have the one without the other. Once apartheid decides that you are "dangerous," you can never be too important to tackle. If they cannot do it by hook, they will do it by crook. Now here I am—in familiar surroundings.

* * * * *

A few minutes after I turned down their breakfast on Monday, November 24, Captain Above-the-Law arrived. If I had not known him, I would have mistaken him for an angel. Dressed in a spotless white or cream-white safari suit and a human face, in a voice of someone going for a holy communion service, he said, without a trace of his usual arrogant self-confidence:

"Please forget about what transpired between us on Saturday morning. It was unfortunate. Please, please, forget about that, Dean. Why did you not tell us that you do not eat our food? We could have arranged something for you."

I stood speechless before this Satan-turned-angel, naked in my gown, among my clothes that were drying on the floor after a haphazard wash that morning. By now, my gown had adapted its color to that of its immediate surroundings: dark brown. When he realized I was short of words, he smiled what seemed to be his innermost feeling of positiveness at that hour, waved and walked away gracefully. Was this man asking for absolution?

When he returned late that afternoon, I was still trying to reconcile the two personalities that were neighbors within the same man: Captain Above-the-Law and Captain Love-and-Forget-It-All.

"Here is your food: rice, cookies, meat, fruits, fish, cool drink. Here is your change of clothes," said Captain Above-the-Law with the confidence of the provident. He gave me a piece of paper on which Regina, my wife, had listed everything she sent, including a few scribbled Scripture passages, and a message of encouragement: "We are praying for you." Above all, I appreciated the Bible, the *Nyimbo dza Vhatendi* and *Phalaphala* hymn books, and the church almanac for daily readings.

"But all clothes must be taken out of the bag; all cool drinks put into a bowl. And fish tins cannot stay with him. These are our regulations," said the young, timid uniformed constable. I immediately took him up on that:

"You can keep the tinned fish for me. But I shall keep my clothes in the bag and the cool drinks where they are. I shall not drink tasteless germ-infested drinks in dirty bowls. If so, you better take them back."

"Okay, we shall speak with the station commander to clarify this issue. In the meantime, let him keep everything." The Captain sounded his most natural—a real Captain Above-the-Law. The poor constable retracted into his shell, and I knew the station commander would bend. Did they want to keep me on my feet for the knockout punch?

I went under the shower. Dressed in clean clothes, I felt like a human being again. During two and a half days of physical and spiritual starvation, I had eaten and drunk very little and read widely—at times wildly—without much concentration. Before the Bible came, I read things scribbled on the walls:

I am Mukumela Denga
Arrested for beating my husband's concubine on July 4, 1980
Appeared in Court on July 10
Released on September 12, 1980.
I shall beat her again.

I am 18 years old
I stole a goat
I liked the meat
They arrested me with two *biltong*[3]
I shall never steal again.

Dear Miriam:
I love you.
I wish you were here.
Hey! I would be mad
One. Two. Three. Four.

Many more obscene writings adorned the walls; but in this world of no books, I was not that choosy. Later I would also make my contributions: dates of interrogations, hospital visits, magistrate's visits, threats, and more. I also played games with or against myself: *muravharavha* (traditional chess) and *ndode* (a traditional stones game for girls). Since I had no stones, I made prison porridge into small round balls, which when dry, became good *ndode* stones.

Physical exercises kept me busy and fit: running in circles in the cell and court; doing push-ups, lying on my back, my buttocks against the wall, my legs raised; or on the mat, making double horse-kicks; raising my arms and dropping them; frog jumping, shadow boxing, and anything that would come to my mind.

In the evening I caught flying ants—something I had not done since I was seventeen—and gave them to common-law detainees the next day through the police. In our community, some kinds of flying ants are a delicacy. Besides sleep and daily prayer devotions thrice a day, the sun kept me busy, as an enemy

3. *biltong:* dried, sliced meat.

and as a friend. In the morning I welcomed its light and lay on the blanket in its warmth; but in the afternoon I kept moving from one part of the courtyard to another, its intensive heat close at my heels. At night I sweated like a horse. The mealtime visits and medicine hours helped break the loneliness, although they occasionally disturbed my daytime sleep.

My first interrogation did not come until Friday, November 28—creating a torturous vacuum of six suspense-filled days.

This Place Is Dirty

It is small
It is square
This place is dirty.

Bucket is toilet
Water in the bucket
Small window at the back
Another far above the door
This place is dirty.

A leaking roof
Wet-smelling blankets
Blackened tasteless coffee
Maize grains with worms
This place is dirty.

Worms in every bite
Phuthu[4] and *phuzamandla*.[5]
A peephole in the door
Blanket dust on the floor
This place is dirty.

4. *phuthu:* hard, crumbling porridge.
5. *phuzamandla:* energy drink.

Light controlled from outside
On and off at Satan's whim
Waking up at siren's call
Blankets folded in a heap
This place is dirty.

Sitting alone in a lonely cell
Admiring beauty in the ugly walls
Here ghosts have footsteps
Footsteps that leave no prints
This place is dirty.

Skik Skik Skik
Bucket Bucket Bucket
Toilet paper on the floor
Not enough for an infant's arse
This place is dirty.

No access to lawyer and family
No access to reason
You sing at a price
You labor for no wage
This place is dirty.

No changing clothes
No soap and face cloth
You speak to yourself
You preach to yourself
This place is dirty.

You sit on nothing
You walk to nowhere
You hear screams by night
You see naked people by day
This place is ugly.

Some are handcuffed in ice-cold water
Women in tattered clothes
Preaching loudly is a crime
Greeting is treason
This place is ugly.

Don't sleep during the day
Don't look innocent without a crime
Exercise is a privilege
Under the shower if you are lucky
This place is ugly.

Humanity is as scarce as gold
Here angels fear to tread
Blankets and clothes are thrown apart
Left scattered without explanation
This place is dirty.

If you are sick,
you'll curse your god;
if you love company,
you'll love yourself;
This place is ugly.

If you count hours,
you'll die before you count days;
if you love arithmetic,
you'll count your toes;
This place is ugly.

If you want interrogation,
you are kept unquestioned;
if you are tired of questions,
the interrogation continues;
This place is dirty.

When you have answers,
you are not asked;
when you do not know,
you must know;
This place is dirty.

When you feel pain,
you must not cry;
when you fail to cry,
you are cheeky;
This place is dirty.

When you confess,
it's all rubbish;
when you vomit nonsense,
peace prevails;
This place is dirty.

When you are tired,
you must not rest;
when you are hungry,
there's no food;
This place is ugly.

When you faint,
you are faking;
if you want to sit,
They make you stand;
This place is ugly.

You want to say no,
they want yes;
you are ready with your yes,
they are ready for your no;
This place is ugly.

Now you are a gentleman,
next minute you are baboon;
you get a smile,
followed by a punch;
This place is ugly.

One of them is black,
but behaves white every way;
you must speak Afrikaans,
good Afrikaans means you think you are white;
This place is dirty.

You were there when you were not there,
when you were there, you were absent;
you meant what you did not say,
you said what you did not mean;
This place is dirty.

You must worship a god you don't believe,
you must believe without faith;
here God is called Satan,
sour is sweet;
This place is ugly.

You want to talk,
but you must write;
you write,
and your statement is shredded;
This place is ugly.

When callous magistrates come,
a smile comes through your tears.
Any problems?
Before you say yes, he's out of sight.
This place is ugly.

You lie bloodied and dying,
and get pills for cold and venereal disease.
Upside down,
you see the land from above.
This place is ugly.

Handcuffed and suspended on a stick between tables,
you cackle like a hen.
Barefoot and naked,
you stand on blunt nails.
This place is ugly.

Long hair and long beard
are all lost in a violent shave.
Frog-jumping for heavyweights,
push-ups without limit.
This place is bad.

In the cold room,
you press the button
when you are ready
to tell "the truth."
This place is bad.

All you know about communism
is the word itself;
here you *are*
communism yourself.
This place is bad.

If accidentally your lawyer and bishop see you,
there's nothing they can do.
Keepers mock your call,
and insult the area below the belt.
This place is dirty.

You miss the love
and embrace of your wife.
Here they call a spade a spade:
black is kaffir and white is baas.
This place is ugly.

It is here that fools are kings,
and the wise obey.
Here postgraduates,
receive instruction from grade-two professors.[6]
This place is ugly.

They are *against* violence
from all that is black;
for violence to preserve
all that is white.
This place is bad.

"If we have to choose
between power-sharing and
wiping you out,
none of you will remain."
This place is ugly.

* * * * *

Roof corrugated iron
Walls zinc all round
On your head against the wall
White punches and kicks land from above and below.
There's death here.

6. Not those who teach grade two, but those who did not go beyond two years of schooling themselves.

Head banged against the wall
Thrown into the air to fall on the concrete floor below
Karate and judo chops and kicks
Total onslaught.
There's death here.

Hit with sticks and chairs
Assailed by muscular men
Bloodied nose, mouth, and knees
Bruised below, above, and everywhere.
There's death here.

"If you are alive by tomorrow,
then we do not know our job."
Behind closed doors and curtains drawn,
Captain R and Sergeant M lead the team.
There's death here.

Naked and handcuffed behind the back.
"Nobody leaves this room alive
unless he says, does the master's will."
By close of day, everything has gone according to plan.
There's death here.

Ankles, wrists, and knees,
eyes, ears, and head,
nose and ribs
have had their share.
There's death here.

You call to God to take your life,
you call on Satan to exercise mercy;
you hate life,
and love to die.
This place is ugly.

You look for God,
and find none;
you lose faith,
and find God.
This place is funny.

You tell lies to uphold the truth,
you withhold the truth to frustrate liars.
You want to die,
and they give you food.
This place is dirty.

You decide to die,
They let you live.
GOD IS STILL IN CHARGE.

14

Incisive Interrogations

I found myself in the familiar torture room: same furniture, same size, same curtains. I saw the floor where I had sat naked and wounded, and I saw the electric plugs. Captain Above-the-Law, now back to his old self, greeted me. My former liturgist—congregant turned torturer—came in, walked around aimlessly, shifted the furniture, pulled out a desk drawer, and glued his right eye on the contents while his left eye surveyed me. I remained indifferent. He drew the curtains and left. By now I had seen at least three of my former torturers on the premises: Captain Above-the-Law, the Liturgist, and the Cucumber, cool and businesslike, who had presided over my 1982 torture. I heard white voices in the adjoining offices but was never allowed a glimpse of their faces.

When the interrogation started, all of my former torturers who were present disappeared into the other offices, and three new faces conducted the interrogation. With few exceptions, all the questions were written. I was given a glass of milk, paper and pen, and the "examination" papers. At the end of the day, I had filled many pages—and they had uttered no bad word. Back in the cell, I did not know whether I had passed or failed the test.

Many more days of interrogation followed, and by mid-December we had covered a wide field: my stand on sanctions, my overseas trips—who financed my tickets and accommodations? how did I get visas? which people did I meet? what did I say? our church delegation discussions with the African National Congress in Lusaka; the burning of Mbeu Bookshop; United Democratic

Front Activities; trade unions; Northern Transvaal Action Committee; why foreign embassy officials visited me and not the homeland government; who bought my cars—recruits for the liberation movement or "terrorist organizations," as they put it; my speeches, sermons, and lectures; my book on the tortures translated into German; the church's and my personal stand on homeland independence; the 1976 boys who were "arrested" trying to cross into Botswana; my relationship with other antiapartheid individuals, such as Pastors Frank Chikane and Molefe Tsele; the Confessing Fellowship, the Community Advice Center, Thusanani Christian Association for the Handicapped; my roles in several overseas conferences on South and Southern Africa, during the visit of the Eminent Persons Group of the Commonwealth and during the U.S. Senate debate on sanctions.

One long Saturday, I was taken through albums of "terrorists'" photos to identify those I knew—and how and why and where I came to know them. After everything was said and done, the interrogations were intensive and extensive, two things that only the security police can combine successfully. The hours varied between five and ten per day, not every day, and only once on Saturday, but never on Sunday. The following Lusaka Communiqué took up about 10 percent of the interrogation time:

November 15, 1986

Dear Brother In Christ

Greetings.

We, Bishop S. E. Serote, Deans T. S. Farisani and C. M. Molefe, Rev. N. P. Phaswana and Mr. D. Nkadimeng, have just returned from Zambia where at the invitation of The Christian Council of Zambia, we were able to make other contacts.

Representatives of Government and the ruling party—UNIP—were gracious enough to receive us. The Director of LWF services there also received us. The historic moment was when the delegation of ANC, with whom we held talks, very warmly received us. Enclosed please therefore find a copy of the joint communiqué, which may give you an impression of the spirit of discussion and the areas of mutual concern.

It was for us a learning experience.

With warm fraternal greetings,

Yours in Christ

BISHOP S. E. SEROTE

JOINT COMMUNIQUÉ OF THE MEETING BETWEEN THE NORTHERN DIOCESE OF THE EVANGELICAL LUTHERAN CHURCH IN SOUTHERN AFRICA AND THE AFRICAN NATIONAL CONGRESS.

On the 12th and 13th of November 1986, delegations of the Northern Diocese of the Evangelical Lutheran Church in Southern Africa and the African National Congress met in Lusaka, capital of the Republic of Zambia. The delegations were led by Bishop of the Northern Diocese of ELCSA, S. E. Serote and Alfred Nzo, Secretary General of the African National Congress.

The meeting was held at the request of the Northern Diocese of ELCSA which was in Lusaka at the invitation of the Christian Council of Zambia. The discussions took place against the backdrop of the escalating conflict in South Africa, characterised by massive repression by the government against democratic forces on the one hand, and a determined struggle by the people on the other. The delegations were at one that the central cause of conflict in our country is the system of apartheid, and that its resolution lay in the creation of a united, non-racial and democratic South Africa.

Such a solution cannot be attained through reform, neither can it be realised without the participation of the African National Congress which is recognised by the majority of South Africans as their genuine representative.

The ELCSA Northern Diocese outlined its platform and the role it is playing in the endeavour to achieve peace and justice in South Africa. As an institution representing a constituency relegated to destitution and untold suffering, ELCSA participates actively in the process to eradicate these evils.

In this regard, the ANC concurred with the view that the Church as a whole has an important role to play in the resolution of the crisis afflicting South Africa. The ANC further explained its policies on a united, non-racial and democratic South Africa.

On reviewing current developments within the country, the delegations noted the importance of the efforts to consolidate the unity of all democratic forces; the campaign to end the occupation of townships and villages by government troops and police; the need for a democratic resolution of the education crisis; the efforts to secure the unconditional release of all political prisoners and detainees; an end to the detention, abuse and indoctrination of children; and united action for the lifting of the State of Emergency.

The delegations further agreed that South Africa is one and indivisible and that any attempts to divide the people on ethnic or other grounds would fail in as much as they only compounded the problems facing the country. The future lies in justice and democracy on the basis of one-person one-vote. This will be achieved only at the instance of united action by all forces opposed to the apartheid regime.

Both sides agreed that the meeting constituted a valuable and historic experience. They agreed to meet again if and when the need arises.

The patterns of questioning varied from day to day, from oral to written, from one interrogator to several at a time, from overfriendly to passionately hostile. A few patterns were fixed: a glass of milk every day, if I wanted it; I always sat, was never forced to stand; written questions came from the invisible handlers next door, and when they could not handle my questions to their questions, they always phoned headquarters. Mr. Headquarters, whoever he was or whoever they were, had an answer to every question. The questions swerved me from heaven to earth, from east to west, from top to bottom, occasionally jolting me from feelings of security to insecurity, from God's protection to vulnerability, from love to hate:

> Dear Dean Doctor T. S. Farisani,
>
> Here are a few simple questions. May you please answer them? When you are tired, tell us, and we shall drive you back to rest.
>
> May God help you!
>
> Amen.

The next minute or the next day, the preamble to the questions would read:

> Dear Farisani,
>
> You son of a witch doctor, professional liar and hypocrite! Answer all the following questions satisfactorily and truthfully or we shall give you the worst V.I.P. treatment ever. We are not the Germans who pay you for your lies.
>
> Come on, you subversive.
>
> We don't care for your prayers!

I protested at these insults and threats on several occasions, and also as part of some of my written statements. I protested at the interrogations, for, I said, I had committed no crime. Also I was convinced that my interrogators were mere police, mere government employees, who understood nothing about politics. We wasted hours on such easy concepts as "human rights," "confederation," justice, ad infinitum. I protested at my continued unjustified detention, which was based simply on my prophetic pronouncements and activities, as well as community development projects. I demanded to be released or charged, failing which I would go on a hunger-strike-to-death.

"Protective" Visits by the Law

The detention laws require that a detainee be taken to a district surgeon immediately after arrest. This had never been done for me during my three previous detentions. The law also requires that a magistrate (or judge) visit a detainee every fourteen days. This is not always taken seriously by either the magistrates or the police, and various reasons are given for every failure: police may say that a detainee has been transferred to another magisterial district, even when that is not true; or they keep moving a detainee from district to district, so that, in fact, he belongs nowhere. Some magistrates have been police themselves, then were promoted to prosecutors, and finally to presiding officers or magistrates. They are not eager to ruffle the comfortable feathers of their former colleagues. What if they used to torture together?

I got regular visits from Sibasa Senior Magistrate Stainer, a former Rhodesian who blamed the death of detainee Isaac Muofhe on the police. Many things I liked about him, positive things that "my" past visiting magistrates did not have. Except for Thursday, January 29, 1987, the day before my release, he came for all his once-every-other-week visits. He had the capacity and, more important, the willingness to listen. He also knew procedure: he would allow neither security police nor uniformed police to be present during our meeting. Only his interpreter—needed or unneeded—always attended, perhaps as a witness. He told the detainee his rights. Without much enthusiasm, he reported on the disposition of previous requests, although at times I had to keep pressure on. Were it not for him, I would never have known that an application for my release was brought in the Supreme Court and rejected, solely on the basis of untested police evidence (see Appendix D).

Stainer took police death threats against me seriously, and he acted. Fortunately, Captain Above-the-Law was one of the police he blamed for Isaac's death, although he was later found not guilty because of "shaky state evidence." When Stainer told me that my request for books for my M.A. studies was turned down, I had no reason to doubt him. But there was his other side: cold, stiff, and officious. As we sat face to face, a big table between us, I could almost hear him say, "But if you were that innocent, why would the police continue to detain you?" I waited for him to say it, but he never did. He also seemed confused about my petition to the minister of justice protesting my detention—in a manner uncharacteristic of him. I was pushed from pillar to post, from magistrate to police. I suspected that there was deliberate collaboration to frustrate my petition, and that pushed me a step further—to go on a fast. On the need for exercise outside the cell once or twice a day, as required by law, he simply said: "The police say they have agreed with your doctors that there is enough exercise space in your cell." No doctor had been to my cell, and in any event, in all my previous detentions, physical exercises were outside the cells, however big or small.

Stainer was totally uninterested in my old torture stories, which became relevant in the light of the latest death or torture threats.

"I am not your lawyer!" he would respond.

"Now, let's say I am tortured tomorrow," I said. "Would you come if I sent for you through the station commander without giving details? Or would I have to wait for your next scheduled visit?" His response sent chilling shockwaves down my spine:

"Remember, Dean. I am not at your beck and call."

"Thank you, your lordship, I have noted in my mind what you said. Now I want you to know that my detention is totally unjustified and unwarranted. It is vengeance for my suit against the police, for exposing my previous tortures, for my stand against apartheid, for my standing suit against top civil servants who wrote a 'deportation petition' against me and two other pastors on February 12 of this year. If I am not charged or released, on January first I shall go on a fast till charged or dead."

"That is your own decision," he said. He picked up his notes; I walked back to my cell.

What has happened to the rule of law in South Africa?

Lord, I Need You Now

Oh Lord my God!
Can a guest become a host?
How does an alien alienate the native?
May a European deafricanize me?

Jesus, oh my savior!
What's Van Riebeeck up to?
Who is P. W. of all the Bothas?
In whose country is the home affairs department?

Oh Lord my God,
Hold my tears lest they fall on foreign soil:
  My guest has turned my history upside down,
  My story he has twisted inside out!

A true brother to the good Samaritan:
I found Botha stranded in the Hague and gave him land,
I found Le Grange wounded and nursed him.
Was it a trap, my Lord?

Heunis was naked and I dressed him,
Viljoen was illiterate and I taught him,
Magnus Malan was afraid and I taught him courage.
Now I must reap the bullets, my Lord?

E. Barber was hungry and I fed him,
Verwoerd was a Nazi and I prayed for him,
Vorster made empty promises and I believed him,
Is every government from you, my Lord?

Treurnicht and Marais were strangers and I housed them,
A few blacks hated whites, and I taught them love,
They pushed me out, I pulled them in,
What are you doing to me, O God?

Christ, my Lord, must we give the other cheek?
Must we go back to the homelands?
Why should they not go back to Europe?
Must we love them while they hate us?

We must be peaceful, you say, my Lord,
While they practice violence every day?
Must we respect their lives, oh God,
While they desecrate our funerals every day?

Must we accept exile like you, my Lord,
Stay in Egypt till the angel's call?
Why not fight our way home,
Or will you take us back today?

We pray for their repentance,
They pray for guns and cannons;
We pray for humanity's freedom,
They pray for white survival.

What's your time, O God?
Past midnight, my God?
Thirty minutes past liberation hour?
Four hundred years past salvation hour?

Shall we take matters into our hands?
Shall we map out our own destiny?
Shall we solve this problem the human way?
Or is there still room for your way?

Oh Lord, Omniscience:
I know I do not know,
I know that I know,
Shall my knowledge alone free me?
I need you to back my know-how,
Of one thing I'm certain: I need you now.

* * * * *

In a white court
Prosecuted by white folk
Before white judges
Using white laws
To defend white interests
In a white world
Full of Herrenvolk
Legal circus.

In a black world
In garments of rightlessness
Where people are guilty at birth
Burdened with Adam's and Ham's sins
And crushed with their own,
We plead guilty before the white judge
For our blackness
But we were not alone
God was also there.

15

At Home in Hell

In one sense, this detention was the most painful, not so much in a physical sense as in its vindictive nature. My guess is that it was more intensive and extensive, and, in interrogation hours, longer than all the previous three combined. Was it because God had foiled the "final solution" on that November 21-22 night? In another sense, this detention had a rare beauty: a lot of food from home (in this sense it was like a hotel); a lot of changes of clothes and toiletries; Bibles—several versions in English, classical Hebrew, modern Hebrew, German, Greek, Venda, and Latin; commentaries in English and Venda; hymnbooks and choruses. Holy communion wafers were allowed, and I had grape juice for wine. My wife sent enough clerical shirts, and I always had a clean white gown. And with the doctors' instructions, clean blankets, pillows, and brand-new mats were provided.

The local uniformed police were, in general, polite: they greeted, laughed, joked, and talked about the weather and latest car accidents. At times they helped the convicts clean my cell, hosing down the ever-accumulating dust and cobwebs from the walls and window meshwires. Between scheduled cleanings, I did it myself—and enjoyed it. They immediately attended to my needs, or they passed my requests on to the station commander, whose sense of responsibility toward me was tempered only by his fear and extreme caution. They rubbed ointments into my legs, arms, back, and chest with the skill of a dedicated nurse. They addressed me as "Dean" or "Mr. Farisani." They admired my library and asked intelligent, interested questions; at times they even asked me to read for them. They accepted my food and ate it with relish. They clearly acknowledged me as their pastor and never made me feel like a "terrorist." Very often they would leave the doors open for a while, never believing that I was the escape type. They helped me keep my humanity—an endangered species in detention. I did not always make their work easy. In the morning, from the station commander and his police—also in the afternoon, evening, and night—came the familiar question: "Any complaints?" Unless I had some special needs or health problems, I always responded in the same fashion: "In prison, away from home and congregations, how do you expect an innocent person to have no complaints?"

A few constables were hopelessly negative: always frowning at me; never greeting me; speaking in one- or two-word sentences: "enough soap?" "broom?" "sick?" "Yes!" "No!" "Tomorrow!" "Don't know!" "Tell them!" "Can't know!" They would either not switch the lights on at sunset, or they would leave them burning the whole hot summer night. They were too busy to bring medicines at scheduled times, or they simply forgot, or they would bring the wrong medicines or the right ones at the wrong time. They did not respect cleaning days, or there was no hosepipe and cleaning cloths, or just not enough convicts to do the job, or it was against the regulations for me to clean my cell. When they came into the cell, they locked the iron grille door behind them; and when they left, they banged the doors, and used the large prison keys to good effect in creating the loudest possible noise. They carried their revolvers or pistols visibly on their bodies, and made me feel "terrorist" the whole way. Surely these are good material for security police! Good recruiting grounds! Good torture squads! Good killers! Good targets for the gospel too!

I reported the medical problems to the station commander, and when that did not help, to the doctor. The security police promised to do everything in their power to correct the anomalies, at times reprimanding the uniformed police in my presence. Some improvements came, but no solution was found until my release. Was there a working agreement between the uniformed and plain-clothes security branches of the police? One playing bad guy and the other good guy? The answer is reserved for Judgment Day.

There were one to three convicted prisoners who worked at the Sibasa Police Station at any given time. They cooked for prisoners awaiting trial and for me, the special prisoner; they cleaned the cells, police offices, police vehicles, and did any other odd job that was required of them. At first they treated me with the utmost caution, and treated the other prisoners as if they were full-time convicts and part-time human beings. When they got used to seeing me, hearing my prayer songs and loud sermons from behind the walls, they gradually opened up and became close friends. I enjoyed listening to their stories as much as they enjoyed mine. I shared my Venda Bible and hymnbooks with them, and part of my food and toiletries. When I was on the fast, I gave them everything. Always through the police. They were always very short-term prisoners; occasionally some stayed for a few days or a week before a relative would pay their fine. Some, I suspect, were being used as traps. I shall not go into detail, but one—among others—told me that he was going home, then came back to my cell many times. Although he did not say it, I could read in his eyes that he wanted me to give him a "secret message" to my family, which he would then hand over to the police.

With the prisoners awaiting trial we shared singing, services, discussions, and many stories—through the walls. I also shared my food with them, of which I had plenty, since I was also allowed to order food with my fifty rand that was in police safekeeping. Almost every weekday I would share in the joy of some prisoners who, on their return from court, would announce their freedom at the top of their voice; but also in the tears of those remanded in custody without bail. One young woman told me, from the neighboring cell, that she was from Vereeniging, a city about 700 kilometers away.

"I was arrested at a roadblock, on my way to visit my husband's family at Vondwe, here in Venda. I am from the Zulu tribe, and I know nobody in Venda. My in-laws do not even know where I am, nor does my husband. After my arrest, a senior police officer took me aside and proposed love to me. Today the prosecutor remanded me to three weeks in custody. The senior officer, now the investigating officer, came to my cell and told me that I know what to do if I want to go home. He pointed to the area between his knees and waist, and said when I am ready I must send for him. I am not used to these things. What should I do?"

I advised her to refuse and report the matter to the station commander. The next day, I heard that she had been transferred to Venda Central Prison. I was never able to establish whether her story was true, how long she stayed in prison, or what happened to her case.

Another man was remanded in custody a day before Christmas—on charges of murder. He was furious and made no attempt to hide his fury and intentions:

"When I am free, I shall blow the prosecutor's head off with a bullet. The magistrate wanted to grant me bail, but he was opposed. Now I must 'eat' Christmas in jail."

I thought to myself: But the man you killed is eating dust; he will "eat" Christmas under the ground.

Love proposals through the walls and the iron grilled courtyard roofs were very common, conducted at the top of the voice:

Man: I am Madanda from Lwamondo. Who are you there?

Woman: I am Phophi from Gondeni. I came last night. Arrested for selling *thothotho.*[1]

Madanda: I beat my wife. She was "going around" me—playing with other men.

Phophi: That is bad of you. You have too much *lulindo*—too strict with your wife. I would never marry you.

Madanda: I love you.

Phophi: You are a woman beater.

Madanda: No. As long as you do not do it before my eyes.

Phophi: You men! But you have many wives!

1. *thothotho:* homemade brandy with a very high alcohol content; it is illegal to brew and sell.

Madanda: Yes. The proverb says: "A man is an elephant, he cannot live on one tree." Another one says: "One wife is like a sister, what can you do with her?" You also know that "a man is a pumpkin, he spreads his branches." Also, what use is "one eye to a one-eyed man when a particle gets into it?"

After describing their looks to each other, they agreed to be lovers. They shared meals and letters through the police. But when the woman was sentenced to a few years and the man discharged, that probably ended the prison high fever called "love."

* * * * *

Except for the threats, insults, and lengthy interrogation sessions, I was never physically abused during this fourth detention. I heard torture screams behind my cell: "I do not know . . . I do not have those things . . . hmm! hmm! yowee, yowee, yowee! I do not know . . . if I knew I would show you. . . ." Occasionally, "mentally deranged" people were locked up in the neighboring cells, and their night-long screams made it impossible to sleep. When I protested, the police denied any knowledge of the screams behind my cell but acknowledged "picking lunatics from the street and locking them up for their own safety." I suggested that Tshilidzini hospital, a mere ten kilometers away, would be the better place for them.

At night mosquitoes poured into the cell through the meshwire and the broken window panes in between. What the police did not do by way of physical abuse, the mosquitoes filled in the gaps. I grabbed the darkness whenever I heard the humming, buzzing wings, and I palmed the walls in hopes of catching them. Before I got cleaner blankets, I had to choose between being a meal for the mosquitoes and covering my body under the smelly blankets in the intense heat. When my wife saw bloodstains on my clothes, she did not suspect the mosquitoes—not after what had happened in 1982!

Every morning mosquito killing was, after my silent prayer, priority number one. I took my sandal and hit tens of them on the wall, leaving blood spots everywhere. It seemed that every day I had more to kill than the previous day! Human beings and insects were allied against me. I felt like despairing and crumbling.

The Fast-to-Death

Before Doctor Zöllner went on leave, I had hinted at a fast-to-death. When I told Dr. Kellermann, he asked me whether I knew the consequences of what I was doing. "Yes," I said. "I know. I followed the hunger strike in Northern Ireland closely; I know every stage."

On New Year's Day, 1987, I gave away all the New Year's food my wife and other friends had sent me: mutton, tripe, fruits, cakes, custard and jelly, fruit juices, and many more. The first four or five days were the hardest, but every additional day thereafter became easier to bear than the one before it.

One afternoon on our way to the hospital, I asked the security police: "Do you hate me?"

When the tension thawed, Blacknut said "No" and sighed heavily. I landed another blow: "Do you love me?"

Another long mile of studied silence, and then, "We do not hate anybody. Why should we hate you? What have you done?"

"Thank you," I said. "I love you . . . God loves you. I pray for you every day."

"Thank you," said Blacknut, "but why do you take your gown everywhere? To our offices? To the hospital? In the cell? We bring you enough clothes, don't we?"

I looked at my gown, played with my cross, and said: "You will not believe me, but I will tell you: this gown, this cross, this clerical shirt and collar, this God who is here but whom you do not see . . . they are all enemies of apartheid and any other evil by man against man. This is my battle uniform—how can I take if off on the front line? Do you understand that . . . do you believe me . . . ?"

All three nodded but said, "We do not know."

As the days wore on, I was wearing down physically and losing weight by the day, but gaining in determination and earning respect from friends and *boereboeties*.[2] My body pains, nightmares, swollen legs and arms, loss of breath, and constipation aggravated my sleeplessness and lack of concentration. The commissioner of police and other senior police waited strategically among old stolen vehicles to get a glimpse of their manmade ghost. I am sure they were happy with their product—and worried.

One day I bit my gum and asked the doctor to talk with me in private. The police officer refused to leave. Doctor Kellermann left to consult the Afrikaner lady superintendent. When it became clear that my request would not be granted I said:

"I want privacy. Doctors must consult in privacy. The police are the cause of my illness. How do you expect me to discuss freely when they are towering over me? You get me privacy, or you stop treating me!"

We left. I expected trouble, but none came. What a Friday!

The next Monday, I was taken to the hospital in the back of a police truck instead of in the beautiful dark Kombi van—unlike previous occasions, with the exception of November 22. Were things back to square one? At the side entrance to the hospital, I was told to sit on the trunk of a fallen tree, under guard, while the team leader went to get my hospital papers. Mathatha Tsedu, a reporter with the *Sowetan Newspaper,* walked slowly past, all the while looking at me stealthily. I greeted him loudly, and when he said "How are you?" I said something like: "This is it. We are struggling. . . ."

Some days or weeks earlier—I was losing track—I had smuggled out a letter of concern to my family and church, including a will to my wife, and announcing my fast-to-death unless charged or released:

> I suspect that this is a revenge detention for exposing my previous torturers to the world, for my stand against apartheid. . . . I am on a hunger strike from New Year's Day until I die unless I am

2. *boereboeties:* friends of apartheid.

> released or charged in a court of law. . . . You should continue to bring food so that they may not have an excuse. At the moment I share it among convicts. . . .
>
> Your loving husband in a dungeon of cruelty. . . .

This Monday I was examined in a side room at a remote wing of the hospital, instead of in the normal Out-Patient Department Consulting rooms. I shared my concerns with the doctor and, among other things, asked for a psychologist for my nightmares. He expressed concern about my hunger strike (which I called a "fast") and encouraged me to take food. I told him that the police had all my answers, the minister of justice had my petitions, and there was no reason why they should not charge me or release me. Did they want to first destroy me mentally and then charge me when I had lost the capacity to defend myself? I would stick to my fruit juices and milk!

When I returned from the toilet, the doctor was engaged in a serious discussion with Blacknut. The next day, my cell was searched thoroughly: my body, clothes, shoes, and socks—nothing escaped their probing fingers. Did the doctor . . . ? God forgive me, but in detention only God can be trusted.

The next scheduled medical appointment date came and went, but nobody took me to the hospital. Instead, a policewoman nurse, wife of a former sheriff, took over my treatment. When ointments ran out she replenished them. Who prescribed them? She took her work very seriously: she came in the morning, she came in the afternoon, in the evening, at night; she felt my pulse and measured my temperature . . . looked into my mouth . . . noted my complaints . . . replaced my ointment—every day, even the day of my release.

The fast went on: I lost appetite. I lost the desire to live. My legs became groggy. I was becoming dizzier and dizzier.

I was losing my balance. I had no desire to talk. At one stage I ate a piece of fish—and cursed my weakness. At interrogations, I drank their milk, but rejected their food.

Here We Stand!

Why probably?
  Possibly!
Why perhaps?
  Maybe!
Scholars fear to take a stand—
Theologians fear to take sides—
Politicians circle issues—
Every person for himself and God for us all.

Why neither yes nor no?
Why neither conservative nor progressive?

Quick at tackling concepts—
Fast at challenging space—
Always slow to call a spade a spade—
One leg in hell, one leg in paradise—
Every genius on a scholastic fence.

When we say God is one, there is no other.
When we speak of God's race, there's no subhuman race.
When we respect our parents, we are right.
When we condemn murder, we are right.
Either we are hot or we are cold.
Either we are boiling or we are freezing.

When we say people are equal, we are right.
When we call for equality of sexes, we are right.
When we condemn discrimination, we are right.
When we right wrong, we are right.
Either we are for or we are against.
Either we approve or disapprove.

When we say apartheid is heresy, we mean it.
When we call for its demise, we don't mean to reform it.
When we call for support, we don't mean slogans.

When we say we shall win, we mean they shall lose.
Either we are winners or we are losers.
Either we pay the price or remain slaves.

When we call for the release of children,
We want to see them free.
When we say *Uhuru* to all,
We want freedom to all.
When we say injury to one,
We mean injury to all.
When we say black is beautiful,
We mean our noses are flat, some flattened.
Either we take a stand or we fall.
Either we become ourselves or shadows of others.

When we say police are beasts,
We've heard them roar.
When we call them murderers,
We can take you to the graves.
When we call them torturers,
We show mutilated bodies.
When we call them Botha's dogs,
We've heard them bark at his call.
Either we call them by name or they'll never know themselves.
Either we say Amen or pray without end.

We are not afraid of 1652.
We are not afraid of Van Riebeeck.
We are not afraid of white paint.
We are not afraid of the SADF.[3]
  We are Africans through and through!
  Before them we were here!
  Next turn we are up! Hope nobody's down?
    Here we stand!

3. South African Defense Force.

16

The Final Three Days

The last three days could be characterized as:

Day One: Polite interrogation.

Day Two: Enthusiastic lectures on politics.

Day Three: Visit to the "Great Mountain."

At the Thohoyandou police headquarters I faced the Commissioner of Police and the Brigadier, Chief of the Security Police, in the former's spacious office. They asked for explanations of my written answers, and as I was busy explaining them during the late afternoon, January 28, 1987, a telephone call came through from Amnesty International or the press in London. I could only hear the responses of the commissioner:

"Farisani is not on a hunger strike. Yes . . . no . . . he is healthy. . . . It is a lie. . . . I know nothing about that . . . that letter is a forgery—he cannot send out letters from prison. . . . No, no, no, nooo!" With his hand still on the telephone receiver, he turned to me: "Did you send out a letter?"

"Yes."

"When?"

"Early in January, I am not sure of the date."

"How?"

"I dropped it through the toilet window at the hospital. I do not know who took it either to the bishop or to my wife."

"Contents?"

"I told everything."

"Names of security police?"

"I do not remember."

"Who gave you the stationery?"

"Your police forgot a pen in my cell, and a small paper."

"But why did you do it? You had told the doctor and the magistrate. That was enough."

"No. I shall be honest with you. If you were me and I were you, and you had gone through what I went through in my previous detentions, you would do exactly the same. In fact, if your police continue to threaten me, you must close all the loopholes or I will smuggle out another one."

"It is bad. We understand. In fact, we can assure you we never authorized those threats."

More telephone calls from newspapers were pouring in like the Levubu River in flood, and the commissioner clearly had some difficulty in handling them. My presence seemed to add to his difficulties.

Later, as I sat with the brigadier, about six tall white men entered the office. The brigadier stood up and saluted.

"You need not salute me, Brigadier," said the tallest of the six. Responding in Afrikaans, the brigadier, himself a hefty man, said:

"I must, I am afraid of you. You are bigger than me." This was clearly meant to be a joke, but I thought there was more to it than met the ear. They all looked at me, then turned and left. They did not greet me when they came in, and they did not greet me when they left. What they discussed I will never know, but later I learned that some were top police and others members of parliament from the "other" South Africa, for we were in the other South Africa, not called South Africa. It reminded me of the Miss South Africa and Miss Africa South beauty contests.[1]

On January 29, both policemen gave me lectures on South Africa and Venda history, and told me that apartheid is something of the past in the "Republic of Venda." We all three agreed

1. To satisfy the demands of the International Beauty Contests Committee, the "government" created two South African titles, Miss South Africa for whites and Miss Africa South for blacks. The latter "country" exists only in the government's apartheid mind.

that apartheid was wrong, but we differed on homelandization as a solution. They were very angry with people who call for sanctions against South Africa: they are guilty of biting the hand that feeds them, they said. They knew that I was a "nonviolent" man, but my speeches were "dangerous though perhaps well-intentioned." Dr. Nkomo of Pretoria made a speech against apartheid, one said. "I was there . . . his audience picked up stones to kill whites . . . they had misunderstood him . . . he called them back to the hall . . . clarified what he meant. . . . You are like that . . . some of your pastors are like that . . . you do not love police . . . we do not hate you . . . we also are against corruption . . . our work is not always easy . . . and . . . and . . . and . . . and . . ."

I hit hard at police persecution of the church, at their plots and traps, the lack of freedom of speech, and the deportation attempt by top government officials the previous year. As long as there is no justice, no truth, no freedom, I said, there will never be peace in our country. They denied involvement in traps and plots. They admitted sending an observer to the "deportation" meeting, but claimed they were not part of it (see Appendix C). I had difficulty accepting their version, for part of my interrogation was about issues raised in the deportation petition to Bishop Serote.

At the end of the day they seemed happy with themselves, and I was happier with God and my groggy self. As I left for the cell, one of them said, "Do not think that we are happy when we sleep in our houses and you in the cell, Dean." Who knows?

That night there was a whirlwind in my mind: Funny: in the cell I am so weak, but during the interrogation I felt very strong. Maybe Christ was right when he said: "Listen! I am sending you out just like sheep to a pack of wolves. . . . Watch out, for there will be men who will arrest you and take you to court, and they will whip you in the synagogues. For my sake you will be brought to trial before rulers and kings, to tell the Good News to them and to the gentiles. When they bring you to trial, do not worry about what you are going to say or how you will say it; when the time comes you will be given what you will say. For the words you will speak will not be yours; they will come from the spirit of our Father speaking through you. . . . If the head of the family is called Beelzebub, the members of the family will be called even worse names!" (Matthew 10:16-25).

My mind also dwelt on the telex from the Lutheran World Federation which reached me on January 8, 1987, offering me work in the United States. Did I respond properly by showing my interest in the offer but stating that I could not decide without consulting my family and the church? Why did the police let the telex through to me? To get rid of me once and for all? Let him howl empty political slogans in Washington and London while we implement our apartheid program at home!

On Monday morning, January 30, I was told to dress properly for a trip. Although no reason was given, I liked the exciting suspense. When Blacknut came, I was already properly dressed and combed: red shoes and cream-white socks, a light grey pair of trousers, a cream-white clerical shirt and collar, my white gown, and on top my cross. I sat in front with Blacknut, a soft-spoken man, while his colleague sat behind in the truck. What a promotion!

When we came to the Justice Department building, the brigadier was waiting in the hallway. He led us in the direction of the Supreme Court, where four years before we had gathered to sue the police for torture. Was it now my turn to stand in the accused's box? Halfway, we turned right, into a large building that houses "parliament" and the "presidency." We walked into the presidency, past Mr. Sinada, my former high school principal, now promoted to Director General of Information, and past Brother Rams, who had participated in my 1982 tortures, into the president's office. The commissioner of police was already there. I sat immediately in front of Thovhele's empty high throne; to my right, a little behind me, sat the commissioner. Directly behind me sat the brigadier. "When the Chief, the great king Thovhele, the Life President arrives, we must all stand," said the commissioner. We did exactly that, and when he had taken his throne, where we all literally looked up to him, we also took our chairs. He had my petition with him.

The commissioner, after the traditional greeting, started the ball rolling: "We are satisfied that he is not a criminal . . . that he is a nonviolent man. . . . Now as we already said it, we thought it proper to let him meet you, *Nemavu*[2] . . . *Ndaa*."

Nemavu said: "We love the church. We have great respect for you, Dean . . . you have been to many countries . . . you have many friends all over the world . . . your friends are our friends. We call all to work together to develop Venda, our country. We do not like trouble . . . or sanctions. . . . No man can fight the church and win. I am also a Christian, baptized in your church. We like peace . . . it is not good to talk bad about our country. There is enough place for all of us. This is your country . . . you can be free in it. . . . I am king for everybody."

I, the prisoner-in-clerical garments, said: "I am happy that we started in prayer. I had initial difficulties praying with the police . . . not with the commissioner and brigadier . . . they, in fact, asked me to pray. . . . I shall be humble but honest with you: they threatened my life; but I shall forgive them. And hope they won't threaten other people. I love you, *Thovhele*[3] . . . God loves you . . . He loves these two . . . He loves everybody. I am not forced by anybody to say what I am saying: I have a God-given responsibility to bring Thovhele and these two to heaven. If you miss heaven, God will ask me why.

"When we correct people in government, they use their power to punish us. But we must do our job as God wills, even if it means correcting these two here. We are happy to hear that you do not like to fight the church; but that is not our experience to date. You heard about the deportation letter . . . now this detention. We all like progress and development; but we love justice more—jobs and equality among all people. If we cannot provide that, we shall need more and more jails . . . which are no solution. I

2. *Nemavu:* owner of the soil, king.
3. *Thovhele:* king (like *Nemavu*).

shall continue to seek an end to apartheid even if that means going all over the world—to Lusaka as well. The gospel calls upon us to work for genuine change . . . and genuine peace . . . based on genuine reconciliation. I am not a 'terrorist'; I am God's pastor. . . . I need not waste your time; Khosikhuhu says it all. If I must die . . . I am not afraid to die . . . but you must know the truth."

Nemavu said: "Take him away, Brigadier." We prayed, and we left the police commissioner where we found him. After some time, he came out and had a session with the brigadier. I did not know which way the cat would jump, but I was at home with my conscience. I knew that Thovhele did not agree with everything I said; but I also saw on his face that he was certain he was not listening to somebody who spent sleepless nights plotting to cut his throat. I also knew that if blacks could be left to sort out their problems without Botha's shadow hanging over them, we could all say: "Apartheid is Satan, and South Africa belongs to us all."

But when I left that office, I had no illusions that we did not have a long way to go. It was a public relations exercise that left the core of the problem untouched: they were happy that I was no "terrorist"; I was happy that my cause was vindicated; but that was as far as it went. *But the mastermind was hiding somewhere in the building in his white skin. And the struggle for justice was raging at the borders and within the country and in every black heart. Ours was a mini-dialogue on mini-issues in an office out of context.*

"We are happy to tell you that today you will sleep at home, Dean," said the brigadier. "After yesterday I could hardly sleep. Now I am happy it is all over. We regret to tell you that Dean Patrick Masekela died two days ago. He is your father. We were always with him. He wanted to see you free. We are happy that you can attend his funeral. You boys, do not forget his mail in that box from the president's office." He was visibly relieved. I thanked him.

"I hope you realize," I said, "that the detention was unwarranted in the first place. Also, I realize that the police who tortured me do not like to look me in the face. Tell them that I do not hold any grudge against them; I am praying for them, and hope they do not do it to another person. My forgiveness is meaningless before God if they continue in their evil. This applies also to those who threatened me during this detention."

They asked me to eat food that my wife brought that day, as she did every day. I turned the offer down, and they loaded the mail box and food into the truck. We collected my personal items from cell number 5, more mail from the torture center, and at about four o'clock that afternoon I saw my mother, my children, and my dear wife dancing in uncontrollable joy. As people poured in that evening, and the telephone line was ringing nonstop, there were jubilation and tears.

Until the next tears!

* * * * *

The next tears were not long in coming. The following interchanges defined my (and my ecclesiastical coworkers') new "in transit" status—and my new identity.

Internal Affairs: We called you to clarify a few issues. Your Bishop Serote and all non-Venda pastors and lay workers and their families will need visas and work permits to operate in Venda. As an independent country, we expect foreigners to have proper documents in our country. Those who need no visas for South Africa, like the Germans, won't need visas for Venda. On their arrival you should immediately notify us.

Farisani: Your predecessor assured us that South African church workers would never be required to have documents. Was that a trap?

Internal Affairs: He was wrong. I know nothing about traps. Excuse me. [He picks up the telephone receiver.] Yes . . . brigadier . . . let us buy an ox for the weekend barbecue . . . it is only six hundred rand . . . that is reasonable . . . Yes, brigadier . . . Yes . . . eh . . . yes . . . yes . . . eh . . . yes. [Dropping the receiver, he turns to me.] You go and do that if you want to promote understanding between the church and the government.

(Back at the church office, by telephone:)

Farisani: Brigadier, what does this restriction order mean? Is it not contrary to the spirit of innocence that you expressed when I was released?
Brigadier: Which letter is that? Where does it come from?
Farisani: From Department of Home Affairs. Pretoria. Dated 28th January. Two days before my release.
Brigadier: That is not from us. That is another department. That is news to me. If you are required to have a visa, go ahead and apply.
Farisani: What about the nonrenewal of Beth Anne Burris's visa by South Africa?
Brigadier: Americans need visas. An enemy of South Africa is also an enemy of Venda. It's as simple as that. We give her just twenty-four hours to leave Venda.
Farisani: That is impossible. She has been with us for a year now. Her home is here. Her personal items and bank accounts are here. How can she wrap that up in twenty-four hours? She is not even here now.
Brigadier: Okay. We shall give her seventy-two hours. That is final. Bye.
Farisani: [on my knees]: There it is, Lord. We all need permits to serve you. This is oppression in the extreme. If man's extremity is God's opportunity, this is it: Your opportunity to intervene.
Amen.

* * * * *

The restriction order was like an ice-cold hammer blow to the center of my head. Not that it was the most crippling order—which it was not. The most painful thing was that, unlike in the past, when the axe had fallen on my friends and colleagues, this time my hour of truth had come. From now on, I would need police permission to move from one piece of my Venda homeland to another—and there are three pieces. To visit parishes in Gazankulu and Lebowa that form part of the Devhula/Lebowa circuit, of which I am responsible as dean, I now required a visa. To attend diocesan and church council meetings, to do work for the Ecumenical Confessing Fellowship and the Governing Board of Church Centers, I now had to apply to the Department of Home Affairs just as foreigners do. If I wanted to go on vacation with my family to Cape Town or Durban or East London, I now needed the blessing of the almighty government. For better or for worse, Pretoria had succeeded in re-creating me into an immobile human unit, joining thousands already so immobilized and blazing the way for thousands who would, one way or another, earn the wrath of Pretoria's disciplinary sword.

One evening I sat in my office thanking God for the thousands of supporting letters and telegrams that poured into the circuit office in my absence. I thanked God for people who care, those who help the oppressed keep their humanity under the most dehumanizing circumstances. I did not feel two threads of tears lazily flowing down my cheeks until I tasted the salty waters at both ends of my mouth, triggering a loud laughter that did little to suppress my anxiety in my new minuscule world.

What will this mean in terms of my health needs? I shall need permission to go back to Johannesburg to complete the tests and treatment by my doctors. It is ironic that, in trying to treat the patient that is apartheid society, I had become a patient myself! Where would I find the Christ who can change this watery existence into wine? He did come—in the form of an invitation to go abroad to meet church leaders and receive medical treatment. But would Pretoria grant the "visa"? How my lawyer and supporting groups managed to wrest that document out of Pretoria's twisted logic is beyond my black intelligence quotient to unravel. But I received it on February 25, 1987, and flew out that evening—through Britain and then to the United States.

The Lord Is My Shepherd
Psalm 23 from the Land of Manna and Quail
November 21, 1986—January 30, 1987

The Lord is my advocate,
I shall never be guilty.
He destroys their every plot,
He removes their traps before my feet.
Besieged and hounded by night,
I shall not give in without a fight.
When Captain Above-the-Law threatens to close my
Mouth once and for all,
Before me unrolls the red carpet of abundant life.
He opens holes on the warrant of arrest,
Letting food in and letters out.
They may win many battles *now,*
The last one will be God's and ours.

Epilogue: At the Crossroads

No Downtown Paradise in the Land of Opportunity

After settling down at the Lutheran Missionary Home Leave apartments in St. Paul, I availed myself of the services of the Minnesota Center for Torture Victims. On March 26, 1987, my family joined me. We all appreciated meeting hundreds and thousands of great American men and women who represent the godly face of the American dream, those who believe in democracy for all humanity and not just for themselves. We met them in church; we met them in human rights groups; we met them in congressmen and women; we met them among laborers, we met them among professionals; we met them in the young, we met them among the old; we met them in the air, we met them on the ground; we met them at demonstrations, we met them at picnics; we met them in their best Sunday suits and costumes, we met them in casual dress; we met them in their true humanity, caring, loving, embracing, praying, and working for freedom wherever people are oppressed in the world irrespective of the nature, color, race, or ideology of the oppressor.

Among these people are the 26,000 who protested my imprisonment to the U.S. State Department in January 1987 alone; the Honorable Congressmen Steve Gunderson, Tim Penny, Ron Wyden; Senator Paul Simon and his colleagues; officials and members of Amnesty International, the Washington Office on Africa, the American Friends Committee, Vukani Mawethu, Tecnica, Southern African Freedom Through Education, Bay

Area Free South Africa movement, Africa Fund, the Lutheran Office on World Community, the Lutheran Church and other denominations. Yes, there is an America out there—a United States of America—that has a human heart and will not rest until all humanity is free. This is the godly face of the dream—the heartening face!

But there is another side of the dream coin, the side that some call a nightmarish face of the dream. A stinging reminder to all who go beyond the shores of apartheid with belief and hope—that beyond the apartheid seas not all is gold that glitters. It does not take long before they discover that beyond Apartheidland live more people who speak Verwoerd's language with a different accent and vocabulary. Some can be excused for lack of knowledge; but many would not qualify to claim ignorance as a mitigating factor.

One can hear them say: "The South African government is not that bad after all. They allow you to come to receive care at the Torture Center. A communist government can't match that mercy. . . . There are reforms everywhere for those who care to see. You now have the Tricameral Parliament, Regional Services Council, President's Council, independent homelands, open sex and open hotels, nonracial sports and . . . who cares? If you people could be more patient, if you could only wait and give your [sic] government more time; if you could stop your natural tendency to throw stones at the police and to burn your own schools; if you could refrain from burning victims with gasoline-filled automobile tires, necklacing innocent, peace-loving people; if you could stop calling for sanctions against your own stomachs through boycotts; if you could discontinue choosing ignorance over knowledge, loving darkness more than light; if you could realize that you burn your feet badly by dancing to Moscow's music, which alienates you from your Christian heritage that puts peace above strife and law above the gospel—you could now hopefully begin to see that the sky would be the only limit. This world . . . your people . . . need conversion born of confession."

Clearly, these hurried observations overlook the 1936 Land

Act that sets aside 87 percent of the land to five million whites, while 87 percent of the population—black—are squeezed into the 13 percent. Since land does not "grow" like a plant, the oppressed are not willing to wait any longer. In fact, they have already waited 400 years and watched in Christian longheartedness as their land has shrunk as fast as their humanity has. Also, what does patience mean for those opponents of apartheid who are in the cold arms of the gallows waiting their appointment with the hangman the next morning?

Detentions and bannings, trials and life sentences, exile life and unmitigated persecution by vigilantes and *kitskonstabels* (antijustice government terrorist squads), disappearances and mutilations, states of emergency, torture and murder—these have not decreased but increased since Sharpeville. The existential question that faces the oppressed is: What human race, what white nation, would—among those prescribing patience—have patience with apartheid? Does not apartheid set the human house on fire? Must those in the burning house wait patiently as those standing at a safe distance counsel long-suffering forgiveness? Concerning that question, Mandela had this to say: "There comes a time in the history of every nation, when there remain only two alternatives, to succumb to oppression or to stand up and fight. We shall not succumb!"

Applauding the tricameral arrangement implies that it is a democratic institution. However, the overwhelming majority of democratic South Africans of mixed blood and Asian background have rejected it as an attempt to make them junior partners in the apartheid political machine and heirs apparent of the criminal record and will for which they are not responsible.

Celebrating the opening up of hotels to "all races" neglects the most basic of mathematical data: in a country where 81 percent of the rural population and 51 percent of the urban population live under the poverty datum line, inviting them to five-star hotels is like instructing a Robben Island life prisoner to kiss his wife through a glass partition. Oppressed people want shelter, food, and clothes, not political gimmicks geared to the gullible racist world which do nothing to correct the fundamental cause of their poverty: racist greed and a false white sense of superiority.

The "sex opportunities" that came with Parliament—three racially segregated segments for whites, colored, and Indian, with the white dominating, the abolition of both the Immorality and the Prohibition of Mixed Marriages acts—continue to elicit enthusiastic approval in White Hall and the White House, but not in Mandelaland and in freedom-thirsty South Africa! This excitement reminds me of a visit to a Louis Trichardt garage that I shall always remember. I had taken my car in for service when I noticed an uncharacteristic, almost "if-you-cannot-make-it-run" glassy look in the garage manager's eye—defeated but unyieldingly triumphalistic:

"You must be very happy . . . very satisfied now. What more do you want? Now you can marry my wife and my daughter. What more do you want?"

I froze, but the manager still confidently expected me to jump in a thanksgiving dance. Unable to bear the steely silence, he walked away shrugging his broad shoulders: "These Bantus do not know what they want. They daily crave to have our women and even report us to the United Nations when we won't share our women. Now we give them our women, and they do not know what to do with them. You may lift a dog on its forelegs, walk a yard or two with it in that position, but when you let go, you have a four-legged animal again—a d-o-g."

Dog or no dog, I remained frozen in a pensive mood. Why not? I was supremely insulted, as were my black brothers. In the first place, what normal man goes around advertising his wife and daughter to other men, and married men for that matter? In the second place—and more importantly—this garage manager implied that the central theme of the Freedom Charter is how to get Afrikaner women. Stretched to its logical mad conclusion, the manager would say that all those forced into exile, all those freedom fighters who died abroad or on the borders of and in South Africa, all those serving long and even life prison terms, all those tortured to death, all those men and women who sacrifice their limited resources and are even willing to make the supreme sacrifice—do so with the main, if not the sole, goal of getting access to the white forbidden fruit.

Not that I am against love and marriage across racial lines—or are they truly lines?—but simply because I cannot persuade myself to congratulate a government on crediting itself for a love affair between two people. We should condemn it for creating those artificial barriers in the first place. If any congratulations are due, they go to those who defied the inhuman "sex laws" and obeyed the higher commandment of love, not to those who spent tax money spying on love across the line, peeping through windows into lovers' most private and intimate moments, breaking down doors and surprising couples at the most innocent and most self-consummating time, inspecting sheets and people's most private areas. The oppressed shall not celebrate.

In fact, those in air-conditioned offices do not know, only those in the oven of apartheid know when the temperatures are low and when they are high; when change is a facade and when it is real; when everything seems changing and the core remains fundamentally unaffected. Hotels? Sex? Sports? Influx control? "What about one person, one vote?" the oppressed ask. In Australia, one person, one vote is democracy; in Europe, one person, one vote is democracy; in the U.S.A., one person, one vote is democracy. In all these instances the majority of voters are white. But when blacks are in the majority—only then does the question of racial domination arise.

The oppressed have decided that in South Africa democracy will also have to mean one person, one vote in a united, democratic, nonracial setting. Why is this democratic pill so difficult to swallow for the authors of democracy now that it must be prescribed and administered by a black doctor? Changing the rules of the game and pushing back the goalposts may delay, even frustrate, the will of the majority for some time, but never forever. Not in South Africa.

APPENDIXES

A

Letters and Documents

The South African government has a limitless capacity for negative creativity and deconstruction of the *imago dei* in black humanity. When it comes to opponents of their racist policies, they never run short of labels and definitions that aim at assassinating their very humanity. If God has performed one miracle in the twentieth century, it is that he has preserved black humanity's humor and smiles in the face of relentless efforts to turn them into beasts: "terrorists" have become presidents and prime ministers, leaders, and decent citizens through the grace of God; buried and banned organizations have unburied and unbanned themselves; "frozen" individuals have thawed themselves out; silenced exiles' voices are heard daily in the streets of Soweto and in the most rural of villages; the voices of comrades Walter Sisulu and Govan Mbeki carry more weight than all those of apartheid's heavyweights combined; Mandela's stature and influence grow by the day, while the Verwoerds, Vorsters, Bothas, and de Klerks of this world slowly—at times perhaps hurriedly—disappear into oblivion.

I do not underestimate the long arm of apartheid. It is still capable of doing untold and incalculable harm to all of us, including, by default, those who oppose it. The fact that Pretoria has failed to create a world of apartheid (make-believe) inhabited by creatures of *Herrenvolk* designs and citizens-of-nowhere is not an unwelcome comedy. We credit God with this victory. I do. We credit the resilience of our imprisoned leaders, whose determination and commitment did not succumb to decades of intolerable deprivation and unacceptable conditions. I do. We credit the men and women and the youth of our country who emerged magnanimous from the state of "boys" and "girls" in servitude through grueling, costly struggles. I do. We credit individuals, churches, politicians and governments, supporting groups, the frontline states, the OAU, the UNO, and the non-aligned movement for their unwavering support in our struggle to be.

When Pretoria's inhumane regime collapses, we hope from the ashes of apartheid will spring forth whites and blacks in the image of God. For South Africa belongs to all who live in it, both black and white. But that day is not here yet; all we see is a promising light at the end of the tunnel. It is not F. W. de Klerk who holds the light; it is God. It is not the *verligtes* (enlightened whites) who will carry us to freedom, though we welcome their tentative willingness to change; it is the oppressed themselves. It is not a light of optimism; it is a light that comes through the sweat of many years of sacrifices and countless battle cries that join Jesus' on the cross: *Eli, Eli, lama sabachtani?* It is the light of a defiant people walking out of the apartheid coffin on Easter Sunday: no more kaffirs hewing wood and drawing water for the self-appointed Shems and Japheths of apartheid.

We see the light from behind prison walls. We move toward the light even through death row. We move toward the light through the obstacles of homeland "self-rule" and "independence." No apartheid darkness, however intense and unyielding, can stop us from following the One who is the way, the truth, and the life.

In the following documents, we hear the true voice of apartheid; we see Pretoria at work trying to make us in its own image. The people of God stand on the way and declare: "In the beginning God created man and woman and called them human beings—Adam and Eve."

* * * * *

[I am grateful to my church for affirming my humanity. The ELCSA (Evangelical Lutheran Church in South Africa) says to me, YOU ARE.]

22 September 1986

To Whom It May Concern:

Our Pastor Dean Farisani will be visiting various countries and will be conducting various interviews.

Our Church is requesting you to grant him safe passage during his travels.

Yours Faithfully,

Mervyn D. Assur

[My wife and my children appreciate our Northern Diocese's affirming our endangered humanity. The Northern Diocese says to me, YOU ARE.]

9 March 1987

The American Lutheran Church
422 South Fifth Street
Minneapolis, Minnesota 55415
U.S.A.

Your Excellency,

On behalf of the Evangelical Lutheran Church in Southern Africa we humbly appeal to you for assistance in the matter of restrictions placed upon our Dean, the Rev. Farisani.

According to the latest development of the withdrawal of possibilities to travel in the Republic of South Africa, he will not attend Diocesan or Church Council meetings, of which he is a member. As convenor and chairperson of several sub-committees in the Northern Diocese he will also not be able to function and serve the church. We want to bring it to your attention that Dean Farisani is Bishop's Deputy in the Northern Diocese.

We kindly appeal to you to use your good offices to persuade the Republic of South Africa authorities to lift this restriction.

Looking forward to your kindest cooperation and assistance.

Yours very sincerely,

S. E. Serote
BISHOP

[The Lutheran World community and all humanity are grateful to the American Lutheran Church for singing the song that affirms my-our-your-endangered humanity. This church says to me, YOU ARE.]

April 1, 1987

Ambassador Herbert Beukes
South African Embassy
3051 Massachusetts Avenue Northwest
Washington, DC 20008

Dear Sir:

We were very pleased to receive the good news that Dean Farisani of the Evangelical Lutheran Church in Southern Africa (ELCSA) was released from detention in Venda on January 30.

At the same time, however, we were deeply distressed to learn that, at the very time of his release, he was served with an order from the South African government restricting him from traveling in South Africa.

According to a letter received on March 19 from S. E. Serote, Bishop of the Northern Diocese and Presiding Bishop of ELCSA, these restrictions will prevent Dean Farisani from carrying out his duties in his own circuit, as well as duties in the Northern Diocese, where he is the Bishop's Deputy, and duties in ELCSA, where he is a member of the Church Council and several other committees.

We find it very difficult to understand that this servant of the Lord, who speaks so openly of love, nonviolence, and reconciliation, and who has never been convicted in spite of four detentions, should be restricted in this manner by a "Christian" government.

When he was detained in Venda, we were told that this was not the responsibility of the South African government but rather of the government of Venda. But this restriction has now been placed on him by the South African government and we urge that this restriction be lifted so that Dean Farisani can carry out his ministry in his area and in other parts of ELCSA.

Yesterday we heard Dean Farisani again speak of his commitment to nonviolence and of his hope and dream that white and black could live and work together in South Africa. When there are persons who are seeking to overthrow the government of South Africa through violence and acts of terrorism, it seems self-defeating that the government of South Africa would seek to restrict a man such as Dean Farisani.

We strongly urge you to do what you can to have this restriction lifted.

Thank you for your attention to this matter.

Sincerely,

Mark W. Thomsen
Executive Director

James L. Knutson
Secretary for Africa

[But Pretoria, like Pharaoh, remains defiant. She continues to try to re-create me in her own image and defines me in a fourfold fashion: Pretoria says to me, YOU ARE.]

28 January 1987

Reverend T. S. Farisani
P. O. Box 314
Sibasa
VENDA

Sir

I have to inform you that your exemption from the visa requirements as laid down in Section 40(1)(c) of the Admission of Persons to the Republic Regulation Act, 1972 (Act 59 of 1972) which you enjoy as a Venda citizen, has been withdrawn. This means that before you can again enter the Republic of South Africa you will have to be in possession of a visa. Application for such a visa may be made to the nearest South African Diplomatic or Consular Representative abroad or to the Director-General, Home Affairs, Pretoria.

Should you in future arrive at a South African port of entry without a visa you will not be permitted to enter.

Furthermore your exemption from the requirements to be in possession of a temporary residence permit in terms of section 2(b) of the Aliens Act, 1937 (Act 1 of 1937) has also been withdrawn.

Yours faithfully

E. Barbes
DIRECTOR-GENERAL

[Closed to church and international pressure, Pretoria persists in stripping me—no, all blacks—of citizenship and all the rights that go with it.]

6 February 1987

REPUBLIC OF SOUTH AFRICA
REF. NO 5545/74 (VL)
ENTRY AND RESIDENCE PERMIT

Permission is hereby granted to Tshenuwani Simon Farisani, holder of Venda Passport no. 000034 issued at Internal Affairs, Venda on the______and valid until 06-02-1990 accompanied by______to proceed to the Republic of South Africa.

This authority is valid for one (1) transit of twelve (12) hours within three (3) months from the date of issue for the purpose of transit to Jan Smuts Airport subject to the holder's passport remaining valid and on condition that he does not without authority from the Director-General, Department of Home Affairs, change the purpose for which he has been admitted, accept employment, engage in any business or profession or remain in South Africa for a visit(s) not exceeding 12 hours.

Issued at Venda on 26-02-1987.

for Director-General
Department of Home Affairs

This document is not valid unless the above photo has been stamped with the official stamp of the issuing office.

[After I regained part of my health at the Minnesota Center for Torture Victims, the world expected the smiling Piet "Promises" Koornhof to come up with the last dregs of apartheid mercy. But on behalf of Pretoria, this was the best he could come up with.]

26 February 1987

REPUBLIC OF SOUTH AFRICA
REPUBLIEK VAN SUID-AFRIKA

VISA/VISUM
No. VE4 22/87 (VL)
Type of visa/Soort visum: Transit

Valid for a single entry on or before 25-05-87 subject to passport remaining valid in compliance with entry requirements and final examination by Passport Control Office at port of entry.

Remarks/Opmerkings: One transit of 12 hours entry to Venda to be assured Ref 5545/74

Issued at/Utgereik te: Thohoyandou
on/on 26-02-1987

AMBASSADOR/AMBASSADEUR

[The Holy Spirit continued to knock at Botha's door of reason and mercy, hoping and trusting that where the two-edged sword had failed, the spirit might succeed. The result was not unpredictable; it was Pretoria's best example of doublespeak.]

3 April 1987

Bishop S. E. Serote
Evangelical Lutheran Church
in South Africa
P. O. Box 1186
PIETERSBURG
0700

Dear Bishop Serote

REV Dean T. S. Farisani

Further to your letter dated 16 March 1987 to the Minister of Home Affairs, I am directed to inform you that the withdrawal of Reverend Farisani's visa exemption does not mean that he is debarred from visiting the Republic of South Africa. Should it, however, be necessary for him to visit the Republic he would have to obtain prior approval from the Department to do so. An application to this effect should be submitted timeously at the South African Embassy Thohoyandou, Sibasa, on the prescribed form BI 84 E, stating also fully the reasons for such a request.

I regret to inform you that your request for the re-instatement of his visa exemption cannot be considered favourably.

Yours faithfully,

(for)
DIRECTOR-GENERAL

Who Am I?

I am not sure about myself,
    And yet
I know them. Strange?
  They are bosses,
  Whites are employers.
  They are clever,
  Whites are skilled.
  They are rulers,
  Whites vote.
  They have farms,
  Whites own industries.
  They have mines,
  Whites are rich.
  They are civilized,
  Whites are Christians.
  They know,
  Whites are pilots.
  They are just,
  Whites are judges.
  They are in charge,
  Whites are engineers.
  They are healthy,
  Whites are strong.
  They are good,
  Whites are superior.
  They are godly,
  Whites are human beings.
      I
know all these;
      they
taught me all these;
      I
am their convert.

      But
Who will tell me who I am?
Pretoria tells me I am not there;

The Church thinks I am becoming;
        But
Who will tell me that I am?
Shall I define myself by my race?
Is this blackness me?
Shall I define myself by positions in
SASO and BPC? Is this dean me?
Do people's definitions define me?
        Hero?
        Brave?
        Courageous?
Coward and brave walk hand in hand in me,
Fear and courage are uncomfortable neighbors,
A man of flesh and of blood,
An heir of hope and despair,
A vessel of hate and of love,
Unwilling clay in the hand of God.
        God
        is
        Spirit
Let me die and define me then.
One day I shall die,
Don't say then I should have stayed on your shores,
For this is a country and not heaven;
  Here people die every day
    As they do everywhere.
      My day must also come
        And I shall die
          Alone.

When duty calls many may dodge,
When heavens call you respond;
There's no such thing as timely death,
  For only One knows the time
  And God's time is timely death.
All we know is that we'll die,
Through God's grace we do well to remember:
these past four hundred years were but
a bonus,

these past twelve years a life
from the dead.
On Pretoria's calendar none of you
should still be here:
You missed the Mandela flight
You missed the Biko train
You missed the Webster excursion
You missed the Solomon Mahlangu final Chicken.

As for me:
I missed the Howich flight
I was not on time for the Masisi Boat
But
When Freedom Airways arrive,
When Humanity's Boat docks,
I
shall cease to bark and shall speak
the-the-the-the-human language.
If this time I am on time,
It's time to go.
If there's no death,
What is resurrection?
If there's no end,
Why should things begin?
If I mourned others,
It is only fair,
That they get their chance,
To mourn over me.

And Christ his chance,
To raise the nation from the dead,
Whose death I share.

B

Congressional Resolutions and Letters

[Black people have wondered over the years whether whites are "convertible" and "convertable" except through defeat, whatever degree of defeat. Why, they ask, should Pretoria defy respectable Congressmen and -women of the United States who have appealed and pleaded?]

100TH CONGRESS
1ST SESSION
H. CON. RES. 26

IN THE HOUSE OF REPRESENTATIVES

Mr. GUNDERSON (for himself, Mr. WYDEN, and Mr. PENNY) submitted the following concurrent resolution; which was referred to the Committee on Foreign Affairs.

CONCURRENT RESOLUTION

Calling for the release of Reverend Tshenuwani Simon Farisani from detention in Venda, a homeland in South Africa.

Whereas Reverend Tshenuwani Simon Farisani, a leader of the Evangelical Lutheran Church in Southern Africa and a spokesperson for that church against the apartheid policies of the South African Government, has testified before the Department of State, the Subcommittee on Human Rights and

International Organizations of the Foreign Affairs Committee of the House of Representatives, and human rights organizations regarding the ill treatment he endured while being detained, in 1981 and 1982, by authorities in Venda, a homeland in South Africa;

Whereas Reverend Farisani is currently being detained by authorities in Venda without charge and for no apparent reason other than the public statements he has made regarding his earlier detention and the need to resolve the current conflict within South Africa;

Whereas Reverend Farisani's life is at risk, as he was severely tortured during his previous detention, has suffered two heart attacks as a result of his ordeal, and is presently on a hunger strike, as a result of which his weight is dangerously low;

Whereas Reverend Farisani has been denied basic civil liberties, such as contact with his lawyer and his wife, and the right to appear at a hearing which was held on December 16, 1986, concerning a petition for his release;

Whereas the detention of Reverend Farisani is part of a pattern of similarly disturbing detentions by South African authorities, including the detentions of Sister Bernard Ncube, Father Hortop, Reverend Molefe Tsele, and Donovan Nadison;

Whereas the detention without charge by South African authorities of persons who express opposition to Government policies violates basic human rights and hinders peaceful solutions to the crisis in South Africa;

Whereas the need is self-evident for all South African leaders to work together to resolve the current crisis in South Africa; and

Whereas the Government of South Africa has significant influence over the leadership of Venda and is capable of intervening on Reverend Farisani's behalf: now, therefore, be it

Resolved by the House of Representatives (the Senate concurring), That it is the sense of the Congress that the Government of South Africa should take the necessary steps to secure the release of Reverend Tshenuwani Simon Farisani from detention in Venda, a homeland in South Africa.

SEC. 2. The Clerk of the House of Representatives shall transmit a copy of this concurrent resolution to the chief of the diplomatic mission of South Africa to the United States.

* * * * *

FROM: Senator Paul Simon/ak

DATE: 01/14/87

RE: Record Statement on detention of Reverend Farisani

Mr. President, we have all heard and read of the great number of human rights violations taking place in South Africa. The accounts of these abuses are so many and so constant that it is easy to become numb to the suffering and misery which so many South Africans are being subjected to every day.

Among the many reports of detention, torture, violence and injustice, there are some cases which stand out and hit us with the full impact of their reality. The detention of Reverned Tshenuwani Simon Farisani in Venda, South Africa is one of these cases.

Reverend Farisani is a South African Lutheran pastor who is internationally renowned for his great faith, his strength of character and his crucial role as a key leader against apartheid. In the late evening of November 21, 1986, 20 Venda security police broke into the Beuster church center. Reverend Farisani, his wife and three children, ages 2 to 7, barricaded themselves in their bedroom for about seven hours before the pastor turned himself over to the police. No one but his captors has seen him since November 22.

This is not the first time Reverend Farisani has been detained by the Venda security police. In November 1981 he was taken into custody and held for two months. During this time he was beaten, abused and treated with electric shocks. As a result of this torture he suffered two heart attacks and was hospitalized for several months when he was released in June 1982.

Reverend Farisani has testified before Congress about the South African situation and his detention experiences. I was fortunate enough to have met with him when he visited Washington in September. I escorted him to the gallery to witness the Senate tell the White House, South Africa and the world that apartheid must end and that the United States should impose sanctions against South Africa until substantive progress is made in the dismantling of apartheid.

Now Reverend Farisani is once again detained and his life is in danger. He has already been sighted in an area hospital at least twice, although prior to his arrest he was neither ill nor injured. Reverend Farisani has begun a hunger strike and is reportedly very weak. Further torture may kill him.

Reverend Farisani's detention is only part of a larger pattern of similarly disturbing detentions which have occurred in South Africa. Father Hortop, a 57 year old Catholic priest, has been detained since June 10, 1986 in a prison in Soweto, South Africa; Reverend Molefe Tsele, an Evangelical Lutheran Church pastor and Publicity Secretary of the National Education Crisis Committee, has been detained since December 12, 1986 when his Johannesburg home was raided; Sister Bernard Ncube, executive and President of the Federation of Transvaal Women, has been detained in Transvaal, South Africa since June 12, 1986; and Donovan Nadison, the Church Youth Work representative on the Youth Council of the World Council of Churches, has been detained since July 7, 1986 in Johannesburg. These are just a few of the many cases of human rights violations in South Africa.

I will be working with Congressman Gunderson on a concurrent resolution regarding Reverend Farisani's detention. I urge all my colleagues to take the time to take a closer look at the increasingly distressing human rights conditions in South Africa and join me in the effort to secure fair and humane treatment for Reverend Farisani.

* * * * *

FROM: Senator Paul Simon

DATE: January 20, 1987

RE: Congressional Record statement

Mr. President, last Friday I mentioned that I would be introducing a Concurrent Resolution regarding the detention of Reverend Tshenuwani Simon Farisani in Venda, a homeland in South Africa.

Reverend Farisani is a leader of the Evangelical Lutheran Church in South Africa. He has been detained without charge since November 22, 1986. Some of you may remember Reverend Farisani from when he visited Washington last fall during the override of the veto on South African sanctions.

He has testified before Congress on the cruel treatment he endured when he was detained in 1981-82. Reverend Farisani suffered two heart attacks as a result of his 1981-82 detention. There are many of us who are very concerned about his health. He has been seen in a hospital since his most recent detention and it is reported that he is on a hunger strike.

This resolution asks the South African authorities to use their substantial influence in Venda, South Africa, to get Reverend Farisani released. Congressman Gunderson has introduced a concurrent resolution on the House side. I urge my colleagues to join me in the effort to bring about the speedy release of Reverend Farisani.

I ask unanimous consent that this resolution be printed in full in the Record.

* * * * *

January 21, 1987

Dear Colleague:

As you know, Reverend Tshenuwani Simon Farisani, a leader of the Evangelical Lutheran Church in Southern Africa, was arrested November 22, 1986, and is being detained without charge by the security forces of Venda, one of the tribal homelands within the borders of South Africa. Since his arrest, he has been denied all contact with his wife, his lawyer, and church officials.

Reverend Farisani has been outspoken in his opposition to apartheid. He has testified here in the United States before the House Foreign Affairs Committee's Subcommittee on Human Rights and International Organizations, and to church groups and Amnesty International chapters nationwide regarding the torture he suffered, in 1981 and 1982, at the hands of the same authorities who now hold him captive. This torture included severe beatings and electric shocks, causing two heart attacks and a permanent limp.

It is absolutely clear that his life is in peril as long as the Vendan authorities detain him. When he was arrested at his home, he told his wife that he recognized one of the security policemen who took him away as the same man who tortured him during his prior imprisonment. Recent reports indicate that Reverend Farisani is dangerously weak due, in part, to a hunger strike he began New Year's Day. He has been sighted at a local hospital nine times since being detained, and his wife has received a parcel of his clothes which included bloodstained nightclothes.

The injustice of this impending tragedy is that Reverend Farisani has done nothing to warrant imprisonment. He has not been accused of any crime or violation of the law, and at present, there are no plans to do so. The Vendan police claim that they are holding him for interrogation. Whatever the rationale, it does not justify the denial of human rights Reverend Farisani is now enduring.

Therefore, we have introduced H. Con. Res. 26, which calls for the Republic of South Africa to take the necessary steps to secure the immediate release of Reverend Farisani from prison. We urge you to join this bipartisan, humanitarian effort to send a clear message to Reverend Farisani's captors of our extreme concern for his safety and well-being and our resolve to continue working for his release. Should you wish to cosponsor or need further information, please contact Kevin Kutz with Representative Gunderson (x5-5506). Thank you for your consideration.

Best regards,

Steve Gunderson, M.C.
Tim Penny, M.C.
Ron Wyden, M.C.

* * * * *

Congressional Record
January 20, 1987

Mr. *Gunderson.* Mr. Speaker, we are all familiar with the litany of tragedy almost daily reported from the Republic of South Africa. We have all been involved, in different degrees, in trying to get all of the leaders of that troubled country to see reason and seek ways toward a peaceful solution to the problems that threaten its future. It is good to know that, although we might disagree as to the best means of change, we all agree that the policy of apartheid is self-destructive, and a severe impediment to the progress of South Africa's people.

My purpose today is to call attention to one victim of this policy, a symbol of the absurd and tragic consequences of a policy of repression. He is Rev. Tshenuwani Simon Farisani, a leader of the Evangelical Lutheran Church in Southern Africa. Early in the morning on November 22, 1986, he was taken from his home and imprisoned by the security police of Venda, one of the tribal homeland states set up and controlled by the South African Government. He was not charged with an offense, no date has been set when he will be charged, a petition for his release has been turned down, and he has been denied contact with his wife and his lawyer.

Reverend Farisani has been outspoken in his opposition to apartheid, and has testified here in the United States before this body's Subcommittee on Human Rights and International Organizations regarding the torture he suffered, in 1981 and 1982, at the hands of the same authorities who now hold him captive. This torture included severe beatings and electric shocks, causing two heart attacks—an unusual thing for a man in his mid-thirties.

As more information is leaked out concerning Reverend Farisani, it is absolutely clear that this gentle pastor's life is in peril as long as the Vendan authorities detain him. When he was arrested at his home, he told his wife that he recognized one of the security policemen who took him away as the same man who tortured him during his prior imprisonment. He has been sighted at a local hospital nine times since his arrest, his wife has received a parcel of his clothes which included bloodstained nightclothes, and he has been on a hunger strike since New Year's Day. Recent press reports claim that he is weakening quickly, and that his weight is dangerously low.

Mr. Speaker, the raw injustice of this impending tragedy is that Reverend Farisani has done nothing to warrant this ill treatment. The Vendan authorities have not charged him. In fact, he has been imprisoned four times before without charges brought against him. He has been held, and is now being held, under the pretext that he is "under investigation." Yet the fact is that the Vendan authorities have not completed their interrogation of Reverend Farisani after 2 months, even though he is currently the only prisoner being interrogated. Whatever the rationale, it does not justify the denial of basic human rights that Reverend Farisani is now enduring. All evidence points to simple harassment on the part of the Vendan authorities.

Therefore, Mr. Speaker, in concert with my colleagues Mr. WYDEN of Oregon and Mr. PENNY of Minnesota, I am introducing a resolution calling for the immediate release of Reverend Farisani, and for the Government of South Africa to take the necessary steps to see that this is achieved. Similar legislation is being introduced in the other body by Senator PAUL SIMON of Illinois.

This is not an opportunity to demonstrate party faithfulness, nor a litmus test to determine adherence to liberalism or conservatism. This is purely a bipartisan, humanitarian effort to release an innocent man from a detention that may very well result in his death. I urge my colleagues from both sides of the aisle to stand with Reverend Farisani by supporting this resolution, and to send a clear message to Reverend Farisani's captors that we, as a legislative body and as a nation, are extremely concerned for his safety and well-being, and will pursue every avenue possible to secure his release.

* * * * *

December 17, 1986

Dear Colleague,

I would like you to join me in signing the attached letter requesting that the government of the Republic of South Africa release the Very Reverend Dean Tshenuwani Simon Farisani, effective head of the Evangelical Lutheran Church in the Venda region.

Reverend Farisani was arrested on Saturday, November 22, 1986, after approximately twenty armed Venda police arrived at the Beuster Mission, where Reverend Farisani is the Minister-in-charge. Reverend Farisani's arrest follows closely on his return to South Africa after a visit to the U.S., sponsored by the International Visitors Program of the Department of State.

As of yet, the Venda authorities have offered no reason for Reverend Farisani's arrest, nor have they disclosed where he is being held or the legal charge for his detention.

In an effort to achieve Reverend Farisani's release, the Department of State has intervened with the South African Ambassador in Washington and also in Pretoria on his behalf. In both instances, the South African authorities claim that they are not responsible. The Department of State has also communicated to the South African authorities that we will hold them responsible for anything that happens to Reverend Farisani.

Reverend Farisani was previously arrested in 1981 and was detained for several months. In testimony that Reverend Farisani made before the Department of State, the House Subcommittee on Human Rights and International Organizations, and Amnesty International, he has stated that he was brutally tortured and ill-treated by Venda security forces. He suffered two heart attacks as a result of his treatment and required prolonged hospital treatment before and after his release in June of 1982.

Under these circumstances, I believe that it is imperative that the South African government, particularly President Pieter W. Botha, know of our concern for the well-being of Reverend Farisani. Please contact Suzzette Allen of my staff at 5-4811 by January 6th if you wish to co-sign this letter, a copy of which is printed on the reverse.

With warm regards,

Sincerely,

RON WYDEN
Member of Congress

C

Report on the Meeting between Adriaan Vlok and a Delegation from the Evangelical Lutheran Church in South Africa

[On September 22, 1989, my church council delegation met the "Minister of Law and Order," Adriaan Vlok, appointed by "reformer" President F. W. de Klerk. The following documents and discussions are illuminating and revealing on both the "determination" of the delegation to fight the case and the government's refusal to lift my restrictions unless I become a pastor in their image.]

EVANGELICAL LUTHERAN CHURCH
IN SOUTHERN AFRICA
REPORT ON MEETING WITH MR. ADRIAAN VLOK:
MINISTER OF LAW AND ORDER ON FRIDAY 22ND
SEPTEMBER 1989: PRETORIA:

The occasion was three fold.

1. To discuss restrictions on T. S. Farisani.
2. To discuss restrictions on M. Tsele.
3. To discuss Police action during Procession of Central Diocesan Rally on 31st July 1989.

Prior to the meeting with Vlok the ELCSA delegation consisting of Bishop M. Buthelezi, Bishop S. E. Serote, Mr. Kgomongwe, Rev M. D. Assur, met at the PMC offices in Pretoria, in a preparatory session. Details of that session is attached as appendix. The discussion with the minister is attached as App 2.

Observation

It is quite evident, in terms of the thinking of the Government that unless preachers toe the line they will not stop the detentions. They would even "write the sermons" if it would come to it. We are expected to apply to Home Affairs for the lifting of the visa restrictions. Law and Order would then give a recommendation. We gained the impression that this would be positive. However, the Church has to undertake to "curb" Farisani in the method and interpretation of the Gospel. The Minister actually said "We will detain him again if he does not stay clear of the political mine field."

We have gained nothing with this exercise and we should thus give no undertaking. Farisani's restrictions must be unconditionally lifted.

Report on Preparatory Meeting to Meet with Mr. A. Vlok: Minister of Law and Order:

Objective: To discuss and strategize for the discussion on the topics of Restrictions of Dean T. S. Farisani and Rev. M. Tsele. And possibly the action of disrupting the Procession of C. D. Rally.

Opening: The Presiding Bishop opened the meeting by reading Psalm 46 and a prayer said by Mr. Z. Z. Mashao. We meet the authorities in the Spirit of Psalm 46.

In Attendance: Bishop S. E. Serote, Bishop M. Buthelezi,

Rev. M. D. Assur, Mr. Z. Z. Mashao (morning only), Mr. A. Kgomongwe.

Preliminaries: Only on one occasion in the past, the authorities have been met on the occasion of Farisani's detention, nothing happened. Another occasion was a meeting of 3 Bishops from Anglican etc. to discuss about the problems in Kwa-Ndebele.

Issue: Taken up by G. A. and CC Executive.

Farisani:
1. Restricted to Venda.
2. Circuit ambit wider than Venda.
3. To apply for a visa every time would be very time consuming.
4. Presently: Studying, lecturing and Public speaking.

He left South Africa to a clinic to receive medical treatment.
R.S.A. requires a visa.
Other Pastors are not required to have a visa.
He serves on various Councils of the Church.
Has been re-elected as Dean.
Bishop's deputy.
Technically the visa issue belongs to the Home Affairs but, connected to detention, that's why we come to the Minister of police. We believe his office can intervene.

1. Thank Minister for opportunity to address him.
2. Farisani was in detention, then released.
3. Then came restriction that he needs visa.
4. Structures of Church relating to deans: Serves on various councils of the Church.

Emergency regulations promulgated for a lot of things but not for religious organizations. Such processions/services have been going on for a long time, breaking up of Church Services.

DISCUSSION ISSUES MINISTER A. VLOK:

1. Detention then release and visa requirements of Dean T. S. Farisani.
2. Restrictions of Rev. M. Tsele.
3. Disruption of Church Procession ELCSA Central Diocese.

Introducing the Issues

1. *Farisani:*
   a. Express thanks and relate also historical aspects with Jimmy Kruger.
   b. That he was detained in Venda, released and then immediately S. A. required him to have a visa.
   c. The work ambit of Farisani in the Context of the Church Structure.

2. M. *Tsele:*
   Due to developments this matter is no longer on the agenda.

3. *Interference with Church Procession ELCSA Central Diocese:*
   Response from Minister's office still awaiting.

Discussion with Minister

The Minister introduced the purpose as G. S. Corresponded. He mentioned that Tsele has been released and is now overseas; so we won't discuss his issue and requested that we address him on Farisani.

Bishop Serote introduced the occasion for meeting with Minister and sketched the background to the Farisani case. Farisani, other than Church activities, was addressed regarding his movements in RSA.

He was not only preaching.
Help to keep Farisani on the straight and narrow road.

Buthelezi: Problem of drawing a line between what is allowable and what is not.
Vlok: You have been able to do that in balance. Preachers deviate in political mine field.
Buthelezi: It's a question of political perception.
Vlok: Yes that's right.
Smit: Would you accept that Farisani can advocate boycotts?
Buthelezi: I am not able to respond in terms of people and perception.
Vlok: Is it acceptable to you gentlemen? I'm sure it's not.
Buthelezi: People have political aspirations in phrasing their views.
Vlok: These issues will now be addressed by the new Government and State president. Farisani is not a sensitive man and this problem I have with him.
Smit: Farisani is a Venda Citizen and restriction against a foreign country.
Serote: We do have question of Farisani for a number of years. Farisani's attitude is a reflection of the past. It is because of the Church's action that the country is not worse than it is. The Church has shared agony for many years.
Vlok: Head of the Church should talk to Farisani so that he does not come into conflict with the Authorities. Undertaking be given to keep Farisani in line if he is allowed to move freely in S. A.
Vlok: I'm not asking that Farisani should not say, 'Apartheid must go.' I'm asking that he should not incite people; he should be a peacemaker.
Smit: Would Farisani come back and address political meetings?
Buthelezi: As we move to a new period, it is necessary to have historical sensitivity in mind. Life comes as a whole and not in pockets, e.g. religious, political, etc.

Vlok: Farisani must be equally sensitive. The way he addresses people. If this happens I have to detain him again. He does not want to create any expectations in the delegation's mind.
A. Kgom: We are not able to say Farisani would be a changed man. Due to what happened to him, he should be a bitter man.
Vlok: If Farisani goes wrong we talk to the Church Delegation; the Church will help. Farisani should apply and the Law and Order Department would give Home Affairs a recommendation.
Vlok: Let bygones be bygones. Maybe this did go wrong. Come back to us on this issue.
Buthelezi: We expect a written reply.
Vlok: A written reply will be sent. He's sorry for happenings.
Buthelezi: Police are in strategic position to interpret what Govt. is saying. We will help how security Police do their work.
Vlok: I would like to ask you to spare a thought for police too. Question to be asked, what attitude do police find in Community—friendliness or what? There rests a great duty on all of us. Pray for Police, tell congregations to help us.

A vote of thanks was expressed by Rev. Assur, who, inter-alia, mentioned that we will have to discuss again with the Minister, regarding the question of Police action. To this he agreed.

D

Mudzunga Regina Farisani's Application for Her Husband's Release

[The following documents demonstrate the black experience of negotiating with "reasonable" white oppressors in Mozambique, Namibia, Zimbabwe, Angola, other places in Africa, and now in South Africa. My wife could not agree more. Pretoria—through Justice Van Rhyn—turned down her application. My wife claimed she knew who I am, but Pretoria claimed to know me better. Black people propose, Pretoria disposes.]

IN THE SUPREME COURT OF VENDA
HELD AT THOHOYANDOU

in the matter between:
MUDZUNGA REGINA FARISANI Applicant

and

THE MINISTER OF JUSTICE 1st Respondent
THE MINISTER OF POLICE 2nd Respondent
THE COMMISSIONER OF POLICE 3rd Respondent

NOTICE OF MOTION

BE PLEASED TO TAKE NOTICE that the applicant intends to make application to the above Honourable Court on the 11th day of December 1986, at 10H00 or as soon thereafter as Counsel may be heard, for orders in the following terms:—

1. Permitting the applicant to make this application without the assistance of her husband and granting her *locus standi* in regard to all proceedings relevant thereto while he is in detention in terms of section 29 of the Maintenance of Law and Order Act No. 13 of 1985.

2. Permitting this application to be heard as one of urgency in terms of Rule 6(11) of the Rules of Court and dispensing with the forms and service provided for in the Rules.

3. Declaring that:—
 3.1 the arrest of Simon Farisani on Saturday 22nd November 1986 at Beuster Mission, District of Thohoyandou, Venda and
 3.2 his subsequent detention in terms of section 29 of the Maintenance of Law and Order Act No. 13 of 1985 are wrongful and unlawful and of no force and effect.

4. Directing the immediate release of SIMON FARISANI.

5. Directing the First Respondent, Second Respondent and Third Respondent forthwith to cause to be taken all measures necessary to ensure that Simon Farisani is not assaulted or ill-treated in any manner whatsoever during such time that he is in detention in terms of Section 29 of the Maintenance of Law and Order Act No. 13 of 1985 or is otherwise in custody of State Officials.

6. Directing that the Respondents pay the costs of this application provided that if any Respondent should not oppose the application such respondent should not be ordered to pay such costs.

7. Granting the Applicant further and/or alternative relief.

FURTHER TAKE NOTICE that the accompanying affidavit of Mudzunga Regina Farisani will be used in support of this application. Kindly place the matter on the roll for hearing accordingly.

DATED AT ________ day of __________ DECEMBER 1986.

ALY LUKOTO
2275 MAKWERELA TOWNSHIP
THOHOYANDOU
VENDA
TEL. NO. 31867
ref: Mr. Aly Lukoto

To: The Registrar of the Above Honourable Court
Thohoyandou

And To: The Minister of Justice
c/o Thohoyandou Government Buildings
Thohoyandou
Venda

And To: The Commissioner of Police
c/o Thohoyandou Government Building
Thohoyandou
Venda.

* * * * *

IN THE SUPREME COURT OF VENDA
HELD AT THOHOYANDOU

In the matter between:
MUDZUNGA REGINA FARISANI Applicant

and

THE MINISTER OF JUSTICE 1st Respondent
THE MINISTER OF POLICE 2nd Respondent
THE COMMISSIONER OF POLICE 3rd Respondent

APPLICANT'S FOUNDING AFFIDAVIT

I, the undersigned

MUDZUNGA REGINA FARISANI

do hereby make oath and say that:

1. (a) I am the applicant in the above matter, of Beuster Mission, district Thohoyandou, Venda.

(b) I am married in community of property to Simon Farisani and I attach hereto as Annexure "A," a copy of my marriage certificate, the original whereof will be produced to this Honourable Court at the hearing of the matter.

(c) By reason of the facts hereinafter stated I respectfully submit that this Honourable Court in the exercise of its discretion will grant me *locus standi* to make the present application and I humbly pray that it do so.

2. (a) The First Respondent is the Minister of Justice, of the Venda Government, Thohoyandou Government Buildings, Thohoyandou, Venda.

(b) The First Respondent is cited herein by reason of the powers that he may exercise in terms of the Maintenance of Law and Order Act No. 13 of 1985.

3. (a) The Second Respondent is the Minister of Police of the Venda Government, Thohoyandou Government Buildings, Thohoyandou, Venda.

(b) The Second Respondent is cited herein for such interest as he may have in this matter.

4. (a) The Third Respondent is the Commissioner of Police of Venda Government, Thohoyandou Government Buildings, Thohoyandou, Venda.

(b) The Third Respondent is cited herein by reason of the fact that he is the senior officer in command of members of the Venda Police.

5. My husband is:

(a) an ordained minister of the Evangelical Lutheran Church in Southern Africa, and a Dean of the Devhula Circuit of the Northern Diocese of the Evangelical Lutheran Church in Southern Africa (Northern Diocese). In this capacity, my husband is the head of the Lutheran Church in the whole of Venda and in areas situated outside Venda;

(b) deputy Bishop of the Evangelical Lutheran Church in Southern Africa (Northern Diocese), and by virtue of this position occupies numerous administrative posts within the Devhula Circuit of the Lutheran Church.

(c) a graduate of the University of South Africa and the holder of the B.A. and the Honours B.A. degrees. He is presently registered as a Masters student with the University of South Africa.

6. (a) On the 22 November 1986 and at about 6.30 am and at our home at Beuster Mission, district of Thohoyandou, my husband was arrested by members of the Venda Police.

(b) This occurred in my presence.

(c) No statement was made by the police to my husband at the time of his arrest as to any offence alleged against him.

(d) I understood from a document which my husband read to me, apparently translating from the Afrikaans language to the Venda language, which document had been handed to him by a member of the Venda Police, that my husband was being detained in terms of the Maintenance of Law and Order, Act No. 13 of 1985.

7. (a) Following upon my husband's arrest as stated above he was taken away from our home by members of the Venda Police and since then I have had no access to him nor have I been informed as to where he is detained.

8. (a) On the 24th November 1986 I visited Brigadier Gerson Ramabulana of the Venda Security Police at his offices at the Thohoyandou Government Buildings, Thohoyandou, Venda, to enquire about the circumstances of, and reason for, my husband's detention.

(b) The Brigadiar did not inform me, despite my requests to him, as to the place where my husband was detained nor as to the reasons for his detention, other than to say that my husband was being held for interrogation in terms of Section 29 of the Maintenance of Law and Order Act No. 13 of 1985.

9. (a) My legal advisers have informed me that in terms of Section 29 of the Maintenance of Law and Order Act a commissioned officer above the rank of Lt. Colonel may arrest a person or cause him to be arrested and detain him, or cause him to be detained for interrogation if such officer has reason to believe that such person has committed or intends to commit certain offences or is withholding from the Venda Police information about this.

(b) I am further informed that the offences relate to terrorism, subversion or the helping of people in regard to such offences or failing to report suspicions about people who intend to commit such offences.

10. (a) I have known my husband since 1972 and we have been married since 1978.

(b) My husband is a critic of the policy of apartheid or separate development and he is opposed to the creation of Black states within the Republic of South Africa; however he does not support the use of violence and has not at any time committed any unlawful acts in furtherance of his political opinion.

(c) He is totally committed to his pastoral work and is a dedicated Christian working for peace.

(d) It cannot be that he is associated in any way with acts of terrorism or subversion or assistance of people who intend to commit such acts.

11. By reason of what I as his wife say and know of my husband I humbly submit that the commissioned officer who caused the arrest and detention of my husband in terms of Section 29 of the Maintenance of Law and Order Act No. 13 of 1985 had no reason to believe that my husband came within the terms of the said Act.

12. (a) My husband was arrested and detained by members of the Venda Police in November 1981 and was not released until June 1982.

(b) It appeared to me from the visible signs on his body and as confirmed by him in reports to me that he suffered torture whilst in police custody.

(c) He instituted an action in this Honourable Court against the police for wrongful and unlawful assault.

(d) The Defendants settled the action by agreeing to pay compensation in the amount of R7 500,00.

(e) By reason of my husband's experience during this earlier detention I verily fear that he may again suffer assault whilst in detention and it is for this reason that I seek on his behalf his protection by this Honourable Court by means of the order stated in the Notice of Motion to prevent any assault upon him by his custodians.

13. I therefore pray for the relief in the Notice of Motion to which this affidavit is attached Section 29 of the said Act.

DEPONENT

SIGNED AND SWORN to before me at ____________ on this the ________ day of DECEMBER 1986 by the Deponent who acknowledged that she knows and understands the contents of this Affidavit, that she has no objection to taking the prescribed oath which she regards as binding on her conscience and has uttered the following words: "SO HELP ME GOD."

COMMISSIONER OF OATHS

E

News Releases

MPHEPHU WARNING TO LUTHERANS

by Patrick Laurence

Patrick Mphephu's quasi-independent state of Venda has threatened to establish its own independent Venda Lutheran Church.

According to an impeccable source in the Lutheran Church, Mphephu loyalists in the Venda regime have written to the Bishop S. E. Serote of the Evangelical Lutheran Church, demanding the recall of three top Lutheran pastors in Venda: Dean T. S. Farisani, Pastor M. P. Phosiwa and Pastor Z. C. Nevhutalu.

Mphephu's men—understood to be top civil servants—have given Bishop Serote until March 31 to recall the clergymen, failing which they have threatened to establish an independent Venda Lutheran Church.

Two of the three clergymen, Farisani and Phosiwa, were detained in Venda following an attack on a police station in Venda in 1981 and the death in detention of a prominent member of the Lutheran Church, Tshifhiwa Muofhe.

The UDI threat against the Lutheran Church follows the detention in Venda of nine men in Venda. All were members of a steering committee of the proposed Northern Transvaal Action Committee and all are said to be members of the Lutheran Church.

Former Transkei President Kaiser Matanzima set a precedent for the establishment of independent churches in the "homelands" when he banned the Methodist Church of SA in 1978 in Transkei and established the Methodist Church of Transkei in its place.

Weekly Mail
March 7, 1986

GET OUT OF VENDA

by Mudini Maivha

Let Our Priests Go, Say Clergymen

Clergymen have pledged support for three Venda priests who have been threatened with expulsion from the area.

This week 28 pastors and church workers in the Devhula-Lebowa circuit—which comprises Gazankulu, Venda and Messina—expressed support for priests Tshenuwani Farisani, Mbulaheni Phosiwa and Zwoitwaho Nevhutalu.

The clergymen rejected an earlier decision by civil servants, who are also members of the church in the area, to have the three transferred.

Clergymen who represent about 12,000 parishioners in the circuit held an emergency meeting at Beauster this week. They rejected the allegations levelled against the three ministers at the meeting attended by civil servants on February 12.

"Church workers have always tried hard to serve their Lord in a hostile environment. And they will continue to do so despite the hardships. Farisani, Phosiwa and Nevhutalu have supported the cause of justice for all, particularly the oppressed. They have opposed apartheid openly and loudly, in various peaceful ways," said the clergymen in a statement.

Top Venda civil servants have demanded the heads of three leading Lutheran pastors—among them internationally respected clergyman Dr. Tshenuwani Farisani.

The civil servants—a former top intelligence official, a poet and several director generals—threatened to establish their own Venda Lutheran Church if Farisani, Zwoitwaho Nevhutalu and Mbulaheni Phosiwa were not transferred to parishes outside Venda.

Last week they gave Bishop Solomon Serote until March 31 to transfer the three.

Farisani—a former SA Students' Organisation executive member and Black People's Convention president—and Phosiwa are both former detainees.

Nevhutalu is the brother of Lusani Nevhutalu, detained for trying to help launch the Northern Transvaal Action Committee.

The bishop refused to reveal the contents of the ultimatum sent to him before he met the signatories on March 14.

He also refused to name the signatories.

But the pastors said they were accused of "terroristic underground and anti-Government activities."

The accusations were apparently prompted by the detentions of Farisani and Phosiwa, and Farisani's anti-apartheid statements at international human rights conferences.

The recent detentions of eight members of the NTACO steering committee—which was to have been launched at the church's headquarters in Beauster on March 1—apparently also influenced the pro-Government members to take the step.

Venda sources said names have already been suggested as replacements for the bishop and the dean in the new church.

Investigations revealed the plot to remove the three church leaders was hatched in Makwarela on March 12.

The plotters have created cells of 10 people in Venda congregations to canvass for their intended breakaway and new church.

Church circles fear if the breakaway occurs, the Government

will ban the present Lutheran Church and force parishioners to join the new church.

City Press
March 9, 1986

ROW OVER LUTHERAN PRIESTS

by Len Maseko

The Lutheran Church's Northern Transvaal parishes are embroiled in a blazing row, which threatens to split the circuit right down the middle.

At the centre of the row are the three Venda priests threatened with expulsion from the Devhula-Lebowa circuit because of their involvement in "terrorist, underground and anti-Government activities." The Devhula-Lebowa circuit comprises Gazankulu, Venda and Messina.

Farisani

The three Lutheran priests are former SA Students' Organisation executive member Dr. Tshenuwani Farisani, Pastor Mbulaheni Phosiwa and Pastor Zwoitwaho Nevhutalu. Venda's civil servants have demanded the three's transfer to parishes outside the homeland.

But a group of pastors and church workers in the Devhula-Lebowa circuit have thrown their support behind the three pastors, threatening that "if they (the three priests) go, we shall all go."

Said the group in a statement: "We shall abide by God's will— not by man's evil desires. An attack on these priests is an attack on all of us in the Devhula-Lebowa circuit, on the diocese in the Evangelical Lutheran Church in Southern Africa and the church of Christ."

"We unanimously support our faithful leaders in Dr. Farisani, Pastor Phosiwa and Pastor Nevhutalu. We call upon all Christians in the circuit to support these God-fearing pastors, to pray for their safety as we do not know what will eventually happen to these three servants of the Lord," the group said.

Venda's civil servants campaigning for the priests' transfer have apparently threatened to establish a new church if their demands are not met. They have sent a petition to the Bishop Solomon Serote, whose decision will determine the future of the circuit as well as that of the three pastors.

Sowetan
March 10, 1986

F

Congregational Letters from Bishop Serote and Dean Farisani

5th/03/1986

CHURCH WORKERS AND CONGREGATIONS
DEVHULA/LEBOA CIRCUIT
(NORTHERN DIOCESE ELCSA)
CIRCULAR NO. 4.

Brothers and Sisters in Christ,

Greetings in the name of the Lord Jesus Christ,

It has come to our attention that there are certain developments in your circuit which can only result in destabilising the church and bringing it into disrepute. We hear that there are "Members of the Lutheran Church in Venda" who want to have your Dean T. S. Farisani, Rev. M. P. Phosiwa, and Rev. Z. C. Nevhutalu transferred out of Venda. The reasons given are grievous indeed. As a church Administration we know that we have a proper constitutional structure which takes care of all matters, concerning individuals, councils, our ministry and an orderly Christian life in obedience to the Gospel. You are therefore being warned against elements and influences, who outside our normal constitutional channels want to disrupt our church life.

We have long gone beyond the stage where we can be manipulated by individuals for personal or ethnic interests. In ELCSA we regard ourselves as brothers and sisters in Christ. Any problems among us are resolved in the spirit of Christ and of Love.

There was a time when you were put under great trial and stress. Your Leader and other pastors were taken away from you, and made to suffer for things they were never found guilty of. You still remember that. Your loyalty and steadfastness in those days is remembered with pride. You remained Loyal to Christ and his church. We know now that we can still depend on you, as faithful and loyal brothers and sisters in Christ.

Let me close by exhorting you to remain vigilant and constant in prayer. I commend you to the reading of 1 Peter 1:3-12.

Yours in Christ,

S. E. Serote
BISHOP

* * * * *

1986-03-10

Evangelical Lutheran Church
Northern Diocese
Devhula/Lebowa Circuit
P. O. Box 314
SIBASA
VENDA
SOUTH AFRICA

Dear Friends Who Care

For many years you have been watching the unfolding of the apartheid drama with concern and anxiety. Now our nation as a whole is beginning to reap the bitter fruits of this anti-man and anti-god ideology. We have reached the crossroads of choice—either down the precipice of apartheid lunacy or up the highway of political justice and social sobriety as the majority of the oppressed have called for, and are now fighting for many years.

In our circuit, which covers Venda, parts of Lebowa and Gazankulu Homelands, the evil forces want to destroy the Church of God, and some of us. They are demanding that we leave the circuit before March 31. Our Diocese, Circuit Council and all our pastors have rejected this evil ultimatum produced at an unconstitutional meeting of between 20 and 30 "Lutheran" top civil servants and security police. They threaten economic sanctions against the diocese and/or the formation of a tribal Venda Lutheran Church unless the bishop transfers these pastors who "are involved in underground antigovernment, terroristic activities."

We have decided to defy this ultimatum irrespective of the consequences.

We ask for your prayers and moral support as we battle this apartheid dragon, declared a heresy by the Church, a political cancer by the UNO, a social dehumaniser by human rights organisations, and an economic murderer by the black oppressed.

May God keep your concern and care for the oppressed burning!

Yours in His Service

Dean T. S. Farisani